INSIDE THE SPORTS PAGES: WORK ROUTINES, PROFESSIONAL IDEOLOGIES, AND THE MANUFACTURE OF SPORTS NEWS

Inside the Sports Pages explores the working world of contemporary sports journalism through the eyes of the reporters, editors, athletes, and media-relations people who inhabit it.

In this first comprehensive study of the work routines and professional ideologies involved in the manufacture of sports news, Mark Douglas Lowes presents a detailed and richly textured ethnographic account of life on the sports desk at a major Canadian daily newspaper. His wide-ranging analysis considers the role of the 'audience commodity' in sports news production, the dynamics of the newsroom, and the complex relations between reporters and their routine sources on the sports beat. The book concludes with an assessment of the ideological nature of sports news, and argues that sports coverage functions primarily as a promotional vehicle for the North American 'major league' sports industry. It will be of interest to anyone concerned about how the media report sports news – and the way they leave some of it unreported.

MARK DOUGLAS LOWES is a doctoral candidate in the School of Communication at Simon Fraser University, where he lectures on sport, media, and popular culture.

MARK DOUGLAS LOWES

Inside the Sports Pages

WORK ROUTINES, PROFESSIONAL IDEOLOGIES, AND THE MANUFACTURE OF SPORTS NEWS

UNIVERSITY OF TORONTO PRESS
Toronto Buffalo London

© University of Toronto Press Incorporated 1999
Toronto Buffalo London
Printed in Canada

ISBN 0-8020-4359-3 (cloth)
ISBN 0-8020-8183-5 (paper)

Printed on acid-free paper

Canadian Cataloguing in Publication Data

Lowes, Mark Douglas, 1969–
  Inside the sports pages : work routines, professional ideologies, and
  the manufacture of sports news

  Includes bibliographical references and index.
  ISBN 0-8020-4359-3 (bound)   ISBN 0-8020-8183-5 (pbk.)

  1. Sports journalism – Canada.   2. Newspapers – Sections,
  columns, etc. – Sports.   I. Title.

  PN4914.S65L68 1998   070.4′4976′0971   C98-932159-2

University of Toronto Press acknowledges the financial assistance
to our publishing program of the Canada Council for the Arts and
the Ontario Arts Council.

This book has been published with the help of a grant from the
Humanities and Social Sciences Federation of Canada, using funds
provided by the Social Sciences and Humanities Research Council
of Canada.

No – not yet. Don't. Stay out here under the moon. You will never, never, have this moment again. It has to last you all your life ...

Timothy Findley, 'Kellerman's Windows'

Contents

viii   Contents

Acknowledgments

I want to begin by thanking George Pollard and Bruce McFarlane for their significant contributions to earlier drafts of this book. Robert Stebbins has become a most welcomed long-distance mentor over the past few years. I'm grateful for the countless hours he has spent reading my work and suggesting new lines of inquiry for me to pursue – all to an anonymous voice over the phone.

I also want to thank Richard Gruneau for giving up so much of his time to read and comment upon several drafts of this book, offering the continuous encouragement and support I needed to see it to its completion.

At the University of Toronto Press, I want especially to thank Virgil Duff for first encouraging me to submit this work, and for championing it through many, many rounds of revision. Thanks also to Barbara Porter and Margaret Williams for their editorial work, to Jill Foran in marketing, and to John St James for his outstanding copy-editing work.

Most important, I want to thank Mom and Dad for all those years they spent enduring butt-freezing Ontario hockey rinks at six o'clock in the morning, and long, rainy autumn afternoons in football stadiums. I'm so glad you were there for me. Rhonda, Jason, and Tara are the coolest siblings going. To my precious little niece, Diandra ... I dream the world for you. And to my uncle, Jim McDermott, I couldn't have done it without you, man.

This book is dedicated in memory of Charles McDermott and Doris Lowes.

Foreword

What little research exists on adult amateur sport indicates that its participants often have a mixed view of their professional counterparts. To be sure, the amateurs almost invariably hold the best of them in awe, marvelling at their superlative athletic feats, the apparent ease with which they execute them, and the tremendous public acclaim that accompanies these two manifestations of excellence. In this regard, the amateurs resemble the general public, which suggests that this assessment of the pros by the amateurs is hardly a surprise. What is less well known and therefore less expected, however, is the dark side of the adult amateur's view of the professionals in his or her sport.

This much more hidden outlook hinges on what is, at bottom, the economic basis of much of modern professional sport. One component of the dark view is the extraordinarily high salaries the top professionals in the most popular team and individual sports negotiate for themselves. On this dimension, the typical amateur is much more likely to identify with the journeymen in the professional ranks: the moderately or even poorly paid enthusiasts who play the game because they love it, just as the amateur does. Very often in the eyes of the latter, the 'fat cat' pros have replaced their desire to play well for the love of it with a desire to get paid well for the lifestyle of it. Strikes in professional sport, the theme with which Mark Lowes opens chapter 1, touch this same nerve in amateur athletes. In their view, it is quite unnecessary to strike when the players are already receiving more than enough money to enable them to devote them-selves on a full-time basis to their profession.

It is, however, the second component of the dark side of the amateur's view of professional athletes that launched Lowes on the research reported in this book, a unique project in the social-scientific study of sport and communications. Many adult amateurs are also greatly miffed at the low to non-existent coverage they receive in the mainstream, big-city sports press. There is, of course, the obvious exception to this observation. This is the coverage of the elite sports, of the Olympic games and the high-level American university team sports, which is of virtually the same order as that of the popular, major-league professional sports. But the rest, alas, receive noticeably less coverage, and the coverage they do receive is relegated to the back pages of the sports section or magazine or the final few minutes, if not the final few seconds, of the sports newscast. As often as not there is no mention at all of what the amateurs did on a given day or weekend, although their playoff and championship games sometimes do marginally better. Some of the adult amateur athletes I interviewed maintained that the local high school teams received more publicity in the media than their own.

Inside the Sports Pages demonstrates that the dark side of the amateurs' view of the professionals in their field is largely, if not wholly, justified. It shows in clear and highly readable terms just how the commercial forces of the day combine in the newspaper world to make coverage of adult amateur sport a bottom-of-the-barrel consideration, good for copy only when nothing else is available to report. But almost always there is something else available. Finally, this book shows that, however it is expressed, no amount of complaining about the matter by the amateurs themselves is likely to have any lasting effect favouring greater or more visible coverage of their games and matches. The modern North American newspaper, in nearly every instance, is a thoroughgoing commercial enterprise, its sports section included, and there is no sign on the horizon of any change in editorial values that might become the basis for adopting a new formula for determining what the printed daily news should consist of.

One might be tempted to ask if *Inside the Sports Pages* itself might not spark a certain amount of change in editorial values. As good a book as it is, my answer to this question is nevertheless an unqualified 'no.' The sports pages and the newspapers of which they are a part have as their economic foundation the venerable and practically immutable institution of modern capitalism. It is most improbable that a scholarly monograph will shake this impregnable fortress. But Lowes's findings could conceivably have a more modest, although hardly insignificant, influence by focusing attention on the oftentimes difficult working conditions of today's sportswriter. On this less lofty level this book might stir the conscience of the occasional sympathizer, who might be in a position to alleviate some of the pressure this person experiences. In the meantime and regardless of whatever practical changes might emanate from it, *Inside the Sports Pages* is a major contribution to the scientific study of sport and communications. Let us hope that this insightful exploration paves the way for further research on the work routines, professional ideologies, and manufacture of sports news.

Robert A. Stebbins
Department of Sociology
University of Calgary

INSIDE THE SPORTS PAGES

Introduction

'I am of the old school,' said he. 'My job is to give the facts, so far as I can discover them, and leave the reader to make up his own mind. I am not in the saint-making business ... I shall offer no opinion of my own.'

I could not accept that. 'Hugh,' said I, 'when it suits you, you slant and load your stories unconscionably. The pretensions of you journalists that you deal simply in fact would be nauseating if it were not laughable.'

Robertson Davies, *The Cunning Man*

It is senseless to talk of an absolute or objective reality without connecting with the *procedures* through which such a reality could be established as real by us.

G.W.F. Hegel

Unprecedented labour strife in 'major league' sport in 1994 created the opportunity for a minor revolution in the sports pages to take hold. For a brief moment in time it seemed that the suspension of play in Major League Baseball and the National Hockey League had forced sports editors to broaden their coverage. In the space of a few months, the front pages of Canadian sports sections went from being the near-total preserve of the big three professional sports – hockey, football, and baseball – to opening up to a new kind of story, like racism in high-school basketball, or the propensity of gymnasts to develop eating disorders.[1]

Once the strike and lockout ended, however, the sports pages quickly resumed their major-league sports bias. In fact, coverage of major-league sport didn't really decline significantly during the shutdowns – it simply changed in nature. Routine game stories and player profiles were replaced with stories (which rapidly became routine in themselves) about the labour strife. Instead of water-cooler talk at the office about Roberto Alomar's brilliant acrobatics at second base, the latest negotiation strategy of the owners became the focus of heated debate.

I started the research for this book with a curiosity about why this is so. Why are the sports pages always so thoroughly saturated with news of the North American major-league sports scene? And why does extended coverage of other aspects of sport seem like such an anomaly when it occurs? For example, in that they garner vastly greater media coverage on a daily basis, what is it about the NHL and the NFL that makes these entertainment spectacles so much more significant than, say, sprint canoeing? What is so engrossing about Major League Baseball players that their every move is breathlessly recounted in the sports pages while elite rowers labour in relative obscurity?

In my view these are important questions. Confronted with them we are forced to stop and think about even more fundamental issues concerning the production of news. Why is it that sports 'journalism' offers such a dearth of investigative reporting compared to the more conventional coverage of politics and business? Why do the media play so completely to the commercial side of sport while largely ignoring so much of the sporting activity that occurs in local communities and regions? Why is it that the media define certain sports as 'major league' and not others?

I want to demonstrate in this book that there is nothing at all 'natural' about this state of affairs – I want to *denaturalize* what is too often taken for granted as immutable. The NBA did not simply evolve into the worldwide entertainment spectacle it is today, nor is there anything natural about the fact that Michael Jordan has one of the most recognizable faces on the planet. Major-league sports and their superstar celebrities are the products of aggressive, multimillion-dollar mass marketing campaigns. They are the products of our mass-media culture – in conjunction with marketing and promotions, extensive media coverage manufactures major-league sports and, to a great extent, our perceptions of them.

It is through the mass media, often thought of as a window onto the world, that we learn about events beyond our immediate experience. Daily newspapers, radio, television – they select, order, organize, and highlight the day's events in a way that tells us what is important, what deserves our attention. The mass media, then, constitute a powerful ideological institution that largely fixes the agenda of public discourse – not telling us *what* to think, but rather what to think *about*. And 'newswork,' which refers to the processes by which news is manufactured, is of principal concern in this regard.

Newswork is the act of constructing reality rather than recording it. Reporters do not simply report events – they participate in them, acting as protagonists. Consequently, the media institution 'affords reporters considerable power as *selectors* of which people can speak in public conversations, as *formulators* of how these people are presented, and as *authors* of knowledge.'[2] Thus, an awareness of how news is produced is indispensable for developing a better understanding of what becomes news and what doesn't, and why this is so.

This book is about newswork and the manufacture of sports news for the daily press. Concerned primarily with work routines and professional ideologies, this ethnographic study of a group of sportswriters explores the social world they inhabit, the people with whom they come in contact, and the pressures and constraints under which they labour. More specifically, this is a study of the methods sportswriters employ in the daily production of news for the sports section of a metropolitan Canadian daily newspaper, the Big City *Examiner* (a pseudonym).[3]

As we shall see, the *Examiner*'s sports newswork environment is shot through with pressures and constraints that directly influence how reporters and editors go about doing their work. The paper's sportswriters in particular have responded by *institutionalizing* various work routines and practices in order to cope with the exigencies of their work.

Just to clarify my terms, by 'institutionalized work routines' I mean a distinctive set of patterns and rules of conduct that persist in recognizably similar forms across long spans of time and space, and represent well-recognized and widely accepted ways of doing things.[4] In other words, today's patterns of action tend to reiterate past patterns. Repeated time after time, these actions become standard operating procedures that take on a life of their own and simply become 'the way things are done.'[5] In this way sports newswork becomes *routine* – a process that has the effect of standardizing sports news, such that day after day it is almost exclusively about a small group of male-dominated professional sports.

Accordingly, the aim of this book is to explore how work routines and professional ideologies determine the content of the sports section of a metropolitan daily newspaper. After all, news is the result of the methods newsworkers employ in their efforts to make sense of 'a buzzing, blooming world of particulars.'[6] Were different methods used to uncover it, different forms of news would result and people would know the sports world outside their direct experience in a much, much different way.

My main argument is that if we want to understand why it is that some sports and athletes enjoy regular and voluminous press coverage and others virtually none, then we must examine the actual processes behind the daily manufacture of sports news. In other words, we have to understand *how* reporters choose what will become sports news, and *why* these decisions are made the way they are.

In recent years researchers in media and cultural studies have argued that news production is most usefully conceived of as a complex circuit consisting of three related moments: the production of news, its circulation, and its consumption (the moment at which audiences consume news and make sense of it). Sports news production in this sense can be conceived of as a dynamic process in which these three moments of the circuit are constantly engaged in the 'production of meaning' among audiences, in the creation of particular ways of seeing and understanding the world of sport. While I acknowledge that these moments are inextricably linked, I want to emphasize at the outset that this study is concerned with the *moment of production* of news for the daily sports press. Even though I do not address the distribution and audience reception of sports news directly, I do examine in detail how audiences and their 'tastes' in sports news are perceived by reporters and editors – which is crucial to understanding the profound commercial sport bias of the newspaper industry.

As for method, this ethnographic account of sports journalism – how it is both practised and experienced by a single group of reporters – is primarily a venture in 'grounded theory.' Grounded theory is an approach to understanding the relationship between theory and data in qualitative research that draws on some of the basic ingredients of analytic induction. The concept of grounded theory was first formulated by Barnie Glaser and Anselm Strauss, in their classic work *The Discovery of Grounded Theory*, as a means of generating theory that is embedded in data.[7] Grounded theories are derived from the fieldwork process, refined and tested during fieldwork, and gradually elaborated into higher levels of abstraction towards the end of the data collection phase.

Following the canons of grounded theory, this study is first and foremost exploratory. Apart from a small handful of scholarly studies, there is a dearth of critical research on the work routines and professional ideologies that underpin the daily manufacture of news for the sports press.[8] It is this paucity of critical work on the subject of sports news production that this study addresses.

As with all case studies, the generality of my findings can be questioned. Nonetheless, the newspaper chosen for study (the Big City *Examiner*) is quite typical of North American daily newspapers. The routine news practices I found at work in the

Examiner's sports department closely correspond with reporters' practices discussed in various sources: biographies and memoirs, magazine and newspaper accounts by former and currently working sports reporters, and the few scholarly works on the subject.

1
Selling Spectacle

In a sense, we have a 50/50 relationship with the media: we can't survive without them and their coverage to the fan; on the other hand, they have a duty to cover us for the fans. So it's a good relationship.

Director of Communications, CFL team

Major-league sports are guaranteed newsmakers – their reach is increasingly global, with hundreds of thousands of people clamouring for information about favourite leagues, teams, and players. Sports teams and leagues work hard to cultivate legions of loyal fans, people who will not only attend events but regularly follow their team's activities with something bordering on religious fervour. And this is precisely why major-league sports depend on intensive media coverage of their activities. This is how they create and sustain such astronomically high levels of public interest in their entertainment product. Media coverage is instrumental in the making of fans, since it is primarily through the mass media that the producers and consumers of sporting spectacle touch each other. In this sense, the mass media are the lynch-pin holding together the various components of the sports entertainment industry.

Now, this is a wonderful state of affairs for daily newspaper organizations, who are in the business of selling their readers to other businesses. Newspaper readers – often referred to as 'audiences' – are a commodity, the sale of which generates the bulk of a daily newspaper's revenue (upwards of 75 per cent). So the more concentrated an audience a newspaper can deliver, the more appeal it has to advertisers and, consequently, the more it can charge for ad space. Major-league sports are ideal in this regard: publishers can count on them to consistently deliver a highly concentrated and easily identifiable *male* audience demographic, a point that I elaborate in much more detail below.

In short, there is a tremendous *synergy* at work among the daily sports press and the components of the major-league sport industry. This chapter explores the nature of this synergistic relationship – how it is forged and sustained, and how it functions to limit the range of sports covered in the Big City *Examiner*. In its quest for a male audience demographic, the *Examiner* restricts its sports section primarily to coverage of major-league spectator sports.

The Major-League Sports Industry

When sport is participant-oriented and played simply for fun and recreation, there is only a passing need to advertise events, publicize results, and interpret what happened – the *raison d'être* of the newspaper sports section. Major-league sport, by contrast, draws its very 'lifeblood' from intense daily media coverage.

In this vein, Dick Beddoes observes that there are 'two branches of athletics: one is played for the game's sake, the other for the gate's sake.'[1] Drawing on Eric Nicol's contention that 'all that bump-and-grind news should not simply be lumped into a section called Sports,' Beddoes argues that the 'bump-and-grind' sections should be split further into 'a page or two of Sports, and a page or two of Athletic Entertainments.' Accordingly, the whole range of professional sports – football, hockey, boxing, horse racing – should be grouped under 'Athletic Entertainments,' since these are, after all, 'investment projects in which the player's purpose is to win for his dear old alma Mammon.' 'On this page ... the writers could fulfill their role as drama critics or as for any other staged performance – hailing the stars, blaming the directors and feeding the fans' appetite for gobbers of gossip.' The 'Sports pages,' by contrast, would chronicle happenings in that 'dwindled field of games that are played *for the fun of it*: cricket, field hockey, college football, amateur curling, swimming.'[2]

Leonard Koppett argues similarly in *Sports Illusion, Sports Reality* that the mass media are necessary vehicles for providing the information that generates massive public interest in, and attachment to, big-time sports.[3] In his view, no commercial sport could be economically self-supporting without extensive media coverage. He notes that when a game or match is over, there are numerous things yet to be discussed: statistics, important plays, records, standings, the overall performances of the players and teams, upcoming games and matches, the rest of the season, next season, and so on. After games or matches have been played, the scores and event highlights become sources of entertainment for fans, whether or not they were able to attend the event in person.

Lawrence Wenner, writing in *Media, Sports, and Society*, makes the point that sporting events are heightened in importance by 'insiders' gossip' about the players and coaches, by speculation on strategy by pundits, and by the historical context for sporting events. 'After a contest has been played, the sports pages recap these same themes, placing the game and its heroes into a "fantasy world" that both sports writers and readers have had a hand in creating.'[4]

The press thus generates public interest in major-league spectator sports by reflecting upon the significance of these spectacles. Media attention fans the flames of public interest in sport, and increased public interest warrants further media attention.

A good case in point is the Canadian Football League in the mid-1980s. As sports historian Frank Cosentino notes, 'If ever a league was immersed in introspection, it was the CFL in 1985.'[5] By this time a host of problems that threatened the very survival of professional football in Canada had surfaced. Foremost among these was an erosion of fan interest, evidenced by plummeting ticket sales. This drop in attendance, according to league commissioner Doug Mitchell, created a perception among corporate sponsors, media, and fans alike that the CFL was simply 'hanging on,' that it was 'minor league' entertainment and no longer a viable professional sports league. One way of changing this negative perception was to reinvent the CFL as a first-rate entertainment spectacle. A planning and marketing committee was appointed; its mission was, in Cosentino's words, 'to set short- and long-term goals for the league and in particular to set a plan of action to turn around the current trend of attendance decline.'

The media stood front and centre in these efforts. Former *Toronto Sun* reporter John Iaboni was hired as director of media and public relations, and he immediately made clear the need to harness the mass media as a promotional vehicle: 'We have a wonderful game with a wonderful tradition and a bright future so the worst thing we can do is to keep all of this a secret when the media is starving for CFL news. The level of reports on the CFL, be it on radio, on TV or in the newspapers, depends on how well we accomplish the task of feeding the news required to assist the media.'[6]

All this is to suggest that, in effect, media coverage is akin to publicity – what I term 'publicity-as-news' – and this is essentially what distinguishes major-league commercial sports from other sporting and recreational activities. It is the major-league sports that have the greatest need for coverage. Copious and regular media coverage creates among fans a sense of caring, of attachment to major-league sports and athletes and even to corporate brand names (e.g., Nike, Adidas). Without this emotion generated by the media, the sports business would collapse.

The point I want to stress here is that the existence of sport does not depend on media coverage. But the continued existence and success of intense major-league sporting spectacle *does*. Again, it is crucial to recognize that the only way the producers of spectacle can reach a critical mass of consumers is through the mass media.

Expansive media coverage is the key to successful sports promotion: the objective is to get people excited about your entertainment product. 'It isn't enough for a promotion to be entertaining, or even amusing: *it must create conversation*.'[7] In this sense, major-league sports organizations attempt to fix the agenda of sports-related public discourse, such that they become the primary topics of sports conversation. 'Sports teams and promoters have learned to manipulate and live within the system and *simply want more ink.*'[8]

'The bottom line is, we want coverage for our team,' explained one media relations staffer. 'You have to maximize the coverage of your team, you know, keep your name in the papers.' For example, during the CFL's 1994 off-season, the *Examiner* reported that the management of Big City's CFL team had been in contact with a former National Football League head coach, now a broadcaster for a major U.S. television network, and were trying to sign him as their new head coach. Although the story was 'bogus from the start,' as one Big City sportswriter put it, it turned out to be a media relations coup for the football club because they had succeeded in capturing headlines for several days – an exceptional feat considering it was the off-season. 'We got a few days of prime coverage ... people couldn't stop talking about it,' said the team's media relations director. As a consequence, the CFL team garnered a great deal of coverage at a time of year when they normally receive little. And since the story ended up headlining sports sections and TV broadcasts across the country, the team had succeeded in making not only themselves but the CFL itself the 'talk of the town.'

Major-league sports organizations want to be in the public light, to be a regular topic of conversation – *they want a lot of ink.* 'The best advertisement in the world is a story in the paper,' acknowledged media relations veteran Gaston Rouge: 'Coverage is really important. You know, it's like free advertising. If you want to pay for an advertisement in the *Examiner*, you're paying, say, "x" amount of cents per word or line. If you get a story written about you that's positive, it's like a free ride ... If you're a PR person who keeps his club in a positive light, then that's all the free advertising in the world for you.' Rouge goes on to draw an interesting parallel between promoting major-league sport and promoting major motion pictures. Both industries depend on *news coverage as a promotional vehicle* for their entertainment products: 'Look at what Disney's doing with the *Lion King* movie. It's unbelievable all the free publicity they're getting for that movie. They're releasing, you know, TV specials about how it was made, the media are doing feature stories on the people who did the voices, who did the music, the songs. When they released the movie, for two weeks in the local papers you had all those stories: but is it really a news story or is it free publicity?'

Ultimately news is valued by major-league sports primarily for its 'instrumental value' in the service of their promotional interests. Major-league sports organizations view the news as a promotional vehicle, a means for generating public interest in, and attachment to their entertainment product. And successful sports promotion hinges on the ability of these organizations to secure routine coverage of their activities in the daily press.

So what do news organizations such as metropolitan daily newspapers get out of this arrangement whereby the big-time sports industry is so dependent on the coverage they provide? As we'll see below, they benefit a great deal. Indeed, the continued existence of the sports section depends on its continuous saturation with news of the world of major-league sport.

The Daily Sports Press

Sport is sold as an entertainment product. Yet insofar as sport is a commodity, it is not the actual content of the sports pages being sold – rather it is the *audience* for that content, the sports fan. In this sense, a newspaper's readership is a commodity, an *audience commodity*, which is sold to advertisers. And it is the relentless pursuit of a primarily male readership that is responsible for the profound commercial sports bias of the daily press. In this section I elaborate this notion of a newspaper's readership as an audience commodity within the context of the rise of the popular sports press in Canada.

The Emergence of the Sports Press in Canada

In his book *The Making of the Canadian Media*, historian Paul

Rutherford argues that perhaps the most outstanding event in the emergence of industrial Canada was the 'renaissance of the popular press.'[9] There was nearly a threefold increase in the number of newspapers published between 1874 and 1900, owing in large part to the emergence of self-proclaimed 'people's journals,' such as *La Presse* (1884) in Montreal; *The Telegram* (1874), *The News* (1881), and *The Star* (1892) in Toronto; the Ottawa *Journal* (1885); and the *Herald* (1889) in Hamilton.

The people's journals, in contrast to expensive 'highbrow' papers, typically sought to shake free of traditional political partisan ties by adopting a more populist stance, producing newspapers geared towards the needs, interests, and reading level of the new urban masses. They began operating increasingly as profit-driven businesses committed to reaching as many readers as possible. By and large, the people's journals were one-cent evening dailies that 'combined sensational practices, maverick politics, and much local news to win the support of the less sophisticated and less prosperous readers in Canada's cities.'[10]

Richard Gruneau and David Whitson, in their book *Hockey Night in Canada*, note that 'the most successful of the new popular dailies experimented with new layouts, increased use of pictures and photographs, dramatic headlines, and sensational stories' to attract readers previously excluded by the highbrow and elitist Victorian press. Moreover, 'they expanded coverage of sports and entertainment, added more cartoons and comics, introduced new columns and whole sections for women; in other words, something for everyone in the whole family.'[11]

The growing representation of popular interests and pleasures in the daily press signalled the new significance of advertising in Canadian popular culture. Publishers were gradually moving beyond their initial use of advertising as simply a supplement to revenues derived from circulation; advertising became the primary moneymaker for these dailies. They realized that their publications were effective vehicles that organized audiences into clearly identifiable target groups that could be sold to advertisers.[12] Audiences themselves became the 'products' generated by the emerging media industry.

Thus, the *quality* of readers became more important than the *quantity* of readers. Newspapers wanted to attract those readers with disposable incomes who could be swayed to purchase an advertiser's wares; consequently, the core market for popular daily newspapers became male wage earners and businessmen.

To help advertisers reach male readers, publishers catered to perceived male tastes in their coverage of politics, business, and labour issues, and, above all, sports. At *La Presse* in Montreal, for instance, the proportion of total news space devoted to political opinions *fell* from about 14 per cent to less than 4 per cent between 1885 and 1914, while space devoted to sports and leisure *rose* from 5 per cent to over 15 per cent.[13] Likewise, in the United States the sports pages had grown into the sports section by the late 1920s, containing much of the same information found in today's newspapers.[14]

Lever and Wheeler's study of the *Chicago Tribune* found that sports coverage became an increasingly significant part of that paper between 1900 and 1975. Sports coverage made up 9 per cent of the total newsprint in 1900 and 17 per cent in 1975, with steady increments for each quarter-century in between. Even more significant was their finding that the amount of sports coverage in relation to general news coverage grew from 14 per cent in 1900 to slightly over 50 per cent in 1975.[15]

By the end of the nineteenth century most major Canadian dailies had substantially increased their sports coverage and created separate sports departments, which divided their attention between local and international, amateur and professional sports.[16] Yet despite this specialization, sports reporting remained strikingly similar to other forms of 'specialty reporting,' and catered to male interests. For example, Rutherford identifies an important similarity between the sports coverage of the era and the press's increasingly specialized coverage of business: 'The two departments boosted their separate pursuits – they thrilled with a sense of the drama and excitement and significance of the little doings of these worlds, never troubling to criticize or question.'[17] In each case, journalists celebrated the ideals of manliness and competition. 'Sports writers glorified the ritualized drama and excitement of masculine physical contests, and business writers exalted the cult of competition in the free market.'[18]

It is in this sense that Gruneau and Whitson argue that 'sports coverage was beneficial not only for building circulation, but also for opening up connections to new sources of advertising revenues from businesses interested in speaking primarily to male consumers.'[19] These new advertising revenue streams included beer and tobacco producers, as well as sporting-goods companies, individual sports promoters, rail and tram companies, and hotel operators.

In a nutshell, daily newspapers sold advertisers access to their sports-section readership, thereby generating the bulk of their revenue. And it is in this context that daily newspapers came to be advertising-supported commercial enterprises. Now, in light of this historical analysis, I'll turn to a more focused discussion of the audience commodity concept and how it has, with little variation, determined the sports content of daily newspapers in both historical and contemporary contexts.

The Audience Commodity

Essentially, the term 'audience commodity' refers to the market relation whereby media audiences are assigned commercial values by media organizations and sold to advertisers. The audience commodity 'plays a central role in the market economy of exchange values in the media industry and constitutes the principal means by which most media organizations are revenue producing.'[20] From the news industry standpoint, the main goal is to consistently produce a high-value audience commodity at a low cost to sell to advertisers in order to maximize revenue and profits. This means producing a highly concentrated and clearly defined audience demographic, something that will appeal to businesses looking to spend their advertising dollars in the most effective publication.

Take, for example, an advertisement by the Canadian Daily Newspapers Association in the 7 November 1929 edition of the

Toronto *Globe*. Under the headline 'The Daily Newspaper Is the Proven Road to Merchandising Success,' the ad explains that in Canada ninety-six newspapers function to satisfy the 'demand of the people of this country for an accurate and complete picture of the news.' Canadian daily newspapers enlist 'time-annihilating' devices like cable, telegraph, and air transport in order that 'millions of Canadian daily newspaper readers may obtain all the news instantly,' thus enabling daily newspapers to 'occupy a position in Canadian life which is filled by no other institution.' Consequently, daily newspapers in Canada are 'by far the most effective advertising media – for both retailer and manufacturer – because of their close, intimate contact with Canadian men and women.'

The advertisement proclaims that, to the retailer, the daily newspaper affords 'concentrated circulation' at the point of publication and in its immediate trading area. To the manufacturer, Canadian dailies offer 'the most economical means of tying up national distribution with national advertising,' permitting 'intensive campaigns and concentrated effort in selected zones.' The advertisement closes by stating that the daily newspaper is the 'keystone of every successful advertising campaign in Canada' – its ability to reach 'all classes, appealing to every member of the family,' produces 'immediate sales results.'

More than sixty years later, little has changed. In the 23 January 1996 edition of the *Globe and Mail*, the paper itself placed an advertisement promoting its ability to deliver 'a million plus readers every weekday.' More important, this readership has '[m]ore high income earners (Personal Income $75K+) and SPBM's (Selected Professional & Business Managers) than any other daily newspaper in Canada.' This audience is 'substantial in size, national in scope, yet powerfully concentrated in urban areas.' Targeted specifically to job recruitment firms (most likely executive headhunting firms), the ad is accompanied by a testimonial from a senior executive at GSI International Consulting Group: 'The *Globe and Mail* is cost-effective. We don't get a huge response. We get a quality response. And that's exactly what we want.'

The point I want to drive home is that financial success in the newspaper industry turns on a paper's ability to deliver *quality* audiences – highly concentrated, homogeneous audiences – in large numbers. This is what Ben Bagdikian calls the 'iron rule' of advertising-supported media: 'It is less important that people buy your publication than they be the "right kind of people."'

Applied to the realm of sport, the 'right kind' of consumers are males eighteen to forty-nine years of age: the demographic category with buying power that may be swayed by the right kind of advertising. As one advertising-industry executive said of this group, 'They may not buy Mercedes, but they buy a hell of a lot of Chevies and Fords.' A newspaper's ability to deliver this highly specific and concentrated male demographic determines whether an advertiser will buy ad space from it. And the prevailing philosophy in the sports news industry is that the best way to attract male readers is with extensive coverage of commercial spectator sports. The sports section allows advertisers to reach men in an atmosphere they enjoy – a paper with a reputation for strong sports coverage will have little trouble selling advertising space to advertisers with an eye on men.[21]

In effect, metropolitan dailies cater to perceived male tastes in order to generate a commercially appealing audience commodity; they do so by providing extensive coverage of commercial spectator sports. The sports pages of metropolitan dailies are thus saturated with commercial sports news, a point underscored by the findings of a number of content analyses.

Joe Scanlon's pioneering content analysis work on the sports pages of thirty Canadian daily newspapers revealed that sports copy consists largely of male-dominated professional sports. A staggering 86.9 per cent of all news items studied could be classified as male; only 5.5 per cent were clearly female (the rest were either 'both' or 'not classifiable').[22] Moreover, Scanlon reports that sports copy was heavily biased towards professional as opposed to amateur sport. During the three-month study period almost two-thirds of the copy (64.9 per cent) was about professional sports, while only 26.8 per cent focused on amateur sports.

Similar findings are reported by Gelinas and Theberge in a more recent study of sports news content in Canadian metropolitan dailies.[23] They conducted a content analysis of sports copy in two Canadian dailies, the *Toronto Star* and Montreal's *La Presse*. In contrast to the extensive coverage of elite professional sport, Gelinas and Theberge found that there was limited coverage of recreational activity (i.e., participant-oriented activity, what may be regarded as 'sport for sport's sake') in these papers.

Not only are daily newspapers lukewarm on community-based sports, but they also demonstrate little interest in women's sports. For instance, Jay Coakley reports that women get less than 15 per cent of the space devoted to sports coverage, and the coverage they do get is less likely to be accompanied by photographs and the in-depth reporting characteristic of major-league sports coverage.[24] Along these lines, Sue Gardener cites a study by the Canadian Association for the Advancement of Women and Sport (CAAWS), based on a content analysis of twenty Canadian dailies during the second week of October, and found that coverage of women in sport dropped substantially from 1995 to 1996.[25] The highest rating went to the Halifax *Chronicle-Herald*, which featured women in 18 per cent of its stories and photographs; the lowest rating, 0.6 per cent, was scored by the Ottawa area's *Le Droit*. Gardener also cites a 1991 four-newspaper study by the Amateur Athletics Foundation of Los Angeles, which found that coverage of professional sports took up 81 per cent of sports sections; and even when professional sports were eliminated from the content analysis, men received nine column inches to every column inch devoted to women.[26]

All this is to drive home the point that major-league commercial spectator sports are 'cash cows' – and newspaper organizations depend on them to 'deliver the male.'[27]

Take the *Ottawa Citizen* as an example. A marketing document I obtained from the paper's research department, entitled 'The New-Look Citizen,' proclaims that the paper offers 'Strengths in Every Section!' – particularly on Mondays when it offers an 'Enhanced Sports Section.' A second document from the same information package reads: 'Every section of the Citizen has its share of interested readers, so no matter where your advertising appears within our pages, you can be assured of excellent results that surpass any other medium.' Supporting figures in the same document announce that '70% of Males Read Sports' and '71% of adults 18–24 Years Read Sports.' More specifically, of the *Citizen*'s 507,900 weekly readers, 54 per cent read the sports section regularly or sometimes over seven days; 63 per cent of these readers are male, and only 37 per cent female. Clearly, the paper's sports section delivers advertisers a highly concentrated and identifiable male demographic.

The television industry also has found commercial sports to be effective vehicles for rounding up male audiences. Television networks develop programs not only with an eye to overall audience numbers, but, more significantly, with a sense of the market segment a particular variant of programming is likely to attract. Each program is in fact the result of a series of market calculations supported by extensive consumer research, whereby a network tries to produce a predictable audience demographic in sufficient proportions to warrant charging a high price for advertising spots during that particular program. This is illustrated by Robert Sparks's study of the development of The Sports Network (TSN), a specialty cable service in Canada.[28]

In its licence application, TSN pitched itself to the Canadian Radio-television and Telecommunications Commission (CRTC) as a general interest sports service, concerned with attracting a broader viewership than the public broadcast networks by offering more regionally and demographically balanced sports coverage. The applicant claimed it would provide a broader, more progressive concept of sports news and entertainment: 'The primary audience target for the service will be people interested in sports. Traditionally the largest demographic segment within this group has been men 18 to 49 years old. Due to the diversity of our program offerings, and to growing interest of both sexes in sports and fitness, we [TSN] would expect to reach a broader spectrum including both men and women of all age groups.'[29]

Sparks argues, however, that TSN's market strategy corresponded more closely to that of public-network sport audiences – those from which it proposed to differentiate itself by offering a 'progressive' alternative.

That the creation of a male audience commodity was TSN's real intention is confirmed by the financial assumptions advanced by TSN in its proposed business plan. Sparks points out that as a precondition for its advertising-revenue calculations, TSN assumed that 'the percentage of males aged 18–49 in the [network's] service subscriber base [would] equal the national percentage.' Moreover, no mention is made in the licence application of women or of other demographic groups typically represented in general interest programming, such as children and young people. TSN's primary audience commodity, therefore, would be a young (early teens) to middle-aged viewer, and the network's advertising-revenue performance would be contingent on amassing a male subscription base and viewing rate that was at least representative of male consumers nationally.

It follows from the above that TSN's programming would concentrate on those professional and elite amateur sports that attract a male demographic, thus marginalizing non-commercial sports, which are often participated in by women and youth. An analysis of TSN's programming record bears this contention out. On the programming-content side of TSN's marketing strategy, Sparks concludes that women viewers have not been well represented. Results of a TSN program analysis between 1985 and 1991 indicate that women's sports events constituted 3.1 per cent or less of total network broadcast hours during this period. Conversely, Sparks found that male athletes, male celebrities and male sports commentators predominated in 94 per cent or more of TSN's programming during the period studied.[30] These numbers are virtually the same as those outlined above regarding the sports press.

Clearly the news industry, be it the daily press or television, genders its sports coverage in the pursuit of advertising revenue. The sports section is a masculine domain, catering to a male audience with whom a male-dominated sporting spectacle has been an immensely effective marketing strategy. News organizations have been able to identify and separate out a male market segment that is especially appealing to advertising interests – in particular, the fast-food, electronics, automobile, beer, and sporting-goods industries. Thus, the philosophy prevailing in the news industry is that the most effective way to attract male readers is to provide extensive coverage of major-league spectator sports – that is, cater to perceived male tastes.

2

Inside the Newsroom

The facts about places, people, and organizations do more than give readers a general familiarity [with the organization in which the research was conducted]. Social organizations work the way the research report says they do only with the right kinds of people and in the right kind of places. So preliminary descriptive materials set down some of the basic premises upon which the report's argument rests.

Howard Becker, *Writing For Social Scientists*

I initially intended to conduct my fieldwork at the Big City *Bugler*, the *Examiner*'s cross-town competitor. In early June 1994, I telephoned the *Bugler*'s senior sports editor, Tom Finnegan, at his home and introduced myself as a university student who was studying sports journalism. I explained that I was specifically interested in learning how the sports section of a metropolitan daily newspaper is put together from scratch each day. I told Finnegan I wanted to immerse myself in the *Bugler*'s sports newswork environment, observing first-hand the work routines of its sports newsworkers. Finnegan expressed genuine interest in this project, indicating there would be no problem with my spending several weeks observing the 'goings on' of the *Bugler*'s sports desk. He told me to call him at work the following Monday morning and we would then make arrangements for me to come in to look around, meet him and his staff, and, in his words, 'get the ball rolling.'

I called Finnegan Monday morning at approximately 11:30 a.m. This is when the problems began. He told me that this wasn't a good week, because 'we're just too busy down here,' and that I should call him early the next week to arrange for my entry into the field. I telephoned him the following Monday morning at approximately 9:30 a.m. – hoping to catch him when he first arrived at his office – and was again stymied: 'I haven't forgotten about you but it's been crazy down here ... Look, give me your home number and I'll call you in a few days when things slow down.'

A week passed and I hadn't heard from Finnegan; so I called him first thing the next Monday morning, at approximately 9:00 a.m., hoping to speak to him before he got too busy. However, no such luck; he was already in meetings. I left a message for him to call me at home when he could. It was late that afternoon before he returned my call, apologizing for not getting back to me earlier but, as usual, he was 'swamped with work all day.'

By this point I had become somewhat frustrated that three weeks had passed since Finnegan had assured me I could begin my fieldwork at the *Bugler*. Without being too aggressive, I indicated to him that it was important for me to begin my fieldwork as soon as possible, given that I was working under a pressing deadline. Finnegan was sympathetic and told me not to worry, that 'we'll get this taken care of soon.' Significantly, Finnegan closed the conversation with yet another promise: 'I'll get back to you as soon as I can. I promise.' He never did call back.

I want to make it clear that I don't think Finnegan was in any way trying to prevent me from observing his paper's sports desk. From the first time we spoke to our last contact, Finnegan was not the least bit put off by the idea of my hanging around the sports desk; he was just too 'swamped' with work to make the arrangements for me to begin my fieldwork.

Even though these events delayed the start of my fieldwork by almost a month, this experience certainly gave me insight into how busy the world of the sports newsworker is. Notice that the factor preventing me from beginning my fieldwork at the *Bugler* was time: 'too busy,' 'swamped,' 'it's crazy down here.' Indeed, rare was the occasion when I called Finnegan at the *Bugler* that I was able to speak to him right away; he was usually in a meeting, talking to one of his reporters about a story, or speaking to someone on the phone. This was my first exposure to the reality that the rhythm of sports newswork is governed by deadlines and a general lack of time, a factor that cropped up repeatedly in my fieldwork.

Because of the difficulty I was having, I decided to see if I could access Big City's other major daily, the *Examiner*. I telephoned Bob Roberts, the paper's sports editor, on the afternoon of 7 July 1994 to see if he would grant me access to the paper's newsroom. I introduced myself in the same manner as I had with Finnegan. And like Finnegan, Roberts was interested in what I was doing; we spent almost forty minutes discussing my project and sports newswork generally. Roberts closed the conversation by telling me I could spend as much time at the paper as I needed, and I could drop by the following Monday afternoon to start.

I arrived at the *Examiner* for the first of several visits at approximately 4:00 p.m. on 11 July. Entering the *Examiner*'s lobby, I was greeted by a receptionist whose small, cluttered workstation was located on the right side of the room. To the left of the foyer I could see the newsroom through frosted glass windows. I informed the receptionist that I had an appointment with sports editor Bob Roberts, and he led me into the newsroom and pointed Roberts out amid the hustle and bustle.

After brief introductions and general small talk, Roberts introduced me to the sports staffers who were present in the newsroom as a university student studying sports journalism. He told them I would be spending a lot of time over the summer 'prowling around the newsroom' and stressed that they should feel free to help me out however they could. Roberts's expansive introduction, because of his status as the senior sports editor, legitimized my presence at the *Examiner*. I had his confirmation that what I was doing was important, and so the cooperation of his staff was needed and, implicitly, expected. In this sense, my route into the *Examiner* was from the 'top-down' rather than from the 'bottom-up.'

Initially, I was concerned that I might run into the same problems as did Richard Cavanagh in his 1989 study of the sports production for CBC television.[1] Cavanagh reports that he was initially treated with a certain amount of suspicion by producers and production staff because of his route into the CBC from the 'top-down'; that is, through the deputy head of TV Sports. Staffers believed that Cavanagh was from CBC headquarters in Ottawa, performing some sort of efficiency rating or audit on the department, and it was a while before their misconceptions were dispelled.

My experience was quite the contrary. The *Examiner* sports newsworkers were genuinely interested in my project. They willingly took time out of their hectic schedules to speak with me whenever I had a question. Not once did I feel I was talked down to, or questioned about a possible hidden agenda in studying sports newswork at the paper. Furthermore, all those interviewed were quite open with their thoughts about, philosophies, and criticisms of commercial sports generally, and of sports newswork specifically.

In the Newsroom

The *Examiner* has a staff of ten sports newsworkers. There are two editors. Bob Roberts is the senior sports editor, and is thirty-five years old. After spending two years in a degree program in physical education, he switched to a journalism diploma program at a community college. He has been doing sports newswork for twelve years: six years as a reporter, and the last six years as an editor at various papers. Jim McDermott is the assistant sports editor. A thirty-five-year-old, he holds a diploma in journalism from a community college and has been doing newswork for thirteen years: eleven as a reporter (nine years in sports and the other two in business/entertainment reporting), and two as an assistant sports editor.

The paper has three sports beat reporters. Buck Colvin covers Big City's National Hockey League (NHL) team. Colvin is a twenty-nine-year-old with eight years' experience as a sports reporter. He holds a journalism diploma from a community college. Bobby Barnes covers the CFL team for the *Examiner* (he also contributes to the NHL beat). Pete Dewey covers Big City's Triple 'A' baseball club. Dewey is a twenty-eight-year-old and has been working as a full-time sports reporter for three years since obtaining his journalism diploma from a community college.

Skip Slider is the paper's regular columnist, well known for his controversial opinions and his daily sports commentaries for a local FM radio station. He is the only member of the *Examiner*'s sports staff that I was unable to interview; Slider writes his columns from home, and since his appearances in the newsroom are rare, he was generally unavailable to interview when I was there doing my fieldwork (nor did he respond to messages I left for him requesting an interview at his home). The other columnist is Tom Lowenstein, a thirty-six-year-old who had been writing his daily column for only about six months when I began this fieldwork. A sports reporter for ten years, he almost completed a degree in journalism from a university, but chose to leave school when offered a full-time sports reporting job.

The *Examiner* has two 'deskers,' who split their time between reporting and preparing the sports section for publication every day. This latter task involves such things as copy-editing, photo selection, and page layout, and occasionally preparing the statistics pages. Sam Snead, in addition to his desker duties, writes a weekly column on network television and sport. Snead is thirty-six years old and has been doing sports newswork for almost fifteen years. He has a diploma in journalism from a community college. Tara Jill is the only female sports newsworker at the paper. In addition to her desk duties, she is a part-time sports reporter.[2]

Finally, the *Examiner* has one freelance sports reporter who regularly contributes stories, though he works on a mostly part-time basis. Chet Burkley is generally responsible for covering Big City's university and college sports scene; he also regularly writes on harness racing. Burkley is twenty-five years old, with a university degree in journalism. He has been working at the

Examiner for four years, first as a copy chaser and now in his present position as a freelancer.

Based on biographical data obtained during interviews, the typical *Examiner* sports newsworker is a thirty-three-year-old white male with about ten years' experience doing sports journalism, and he holds a diploma in journalism from a community college.

The Newsroom Layout

An interesting feature of the layout of the *Examiner*'s newsroom is the economy of space: every area is utilized for the production of news. *Ceilings* all have numerous television sets suspended from them so reporters can watch news programs throughout the day and evening. When asked about this set-up, one reporter explained why newsworkers 'religiously' watch television newscasts. 'Just to see if any news has broken, you know, make sure we haven't missed a story ... We like to know how the [local television stations] are handling a story.'[3]

Wall space doubles as a bulletin board, with posters and notes pasted all over. *Floor space* is also fully utilized. Reporters' workstations, which are basically small cubicles, line every wall and stretch straight down the middle of the newsroom in aisles. Each cubicle is sparsely furnished with a chair, a telephone, and an extremely old-looking computer terminal. These computers were not only old, but of poor quality, obviously pushed well beyond their years of optimum performance. I witnessed three occasions when sports reporters lost stories they were working on owing to computer malfunction. This apparently is a regular occurrence: 'Oh, it happens all the time. I lose a story probably two or three times a week, you just get used to it. We had better computers at journalism school.' Even the space in these workstations is fully utilized. Cubicle desks are littered with press releases, media guides, and other such printed material; the walls are plastered with pieces of paper, the information appearing to be mostly telephone numbers, statistics, and reminders of various sorts. The clutter of most workstations is an apt symbol for the chaotic newswork environment at the *Examiner*, which I describe below.

One striking feature of these workstations is the lack of privacy; the walls separating the cubicles are only shoulder-high when a person is sitting down. I asked Roberts, the sports editor, about this, wondering whether the lack of privacy makes it difficult to concentrate: 'Not really. They're always talking to each other, exchanging information, asking questions. If we had walls reaching to the ceiling or private offices or whatever, you would obviously lose this open space which is key to communication.' What Roberts implies here is that newsmaking is a creative process that encourages, to a fairly high degree, collaboration among newsworkers in the making of news – a sharing of information and ideas. In short, the newsroom layout contributes to the creative process behind news manufacture. Just as important, by facilitating a collaborative atmosphere, the layout helps sports reporters generate news in a pressure-filled environment where deadlines always loom.

Sports newswork at the *Examiner* is carried out at a very hectic pace. To an outsider's first glance, activity in the newsroom seems completely incoherent, a senseless flurry of confusion akin to the organized chaos which marks activity on the floor of the Toronto or New York Stock Exchanges, or in an ant colony. Sports newsworkers typically work a 3 p.m. to 11 p.m. shift, and as the evening wears on and the deadline approaches the pace picks up. As reporters scramble to finish their stories, and editors and deskers await these news items so they can lay out the sports pages, a constant barrage of questions and orders pounds the ears – 'Who pitched for the Jays last night? What's his ERA?'; 'Do you know if Barrett is starting tonight or is he still benched?'; 'Hey Colvin! What's going on with Turlotte? Can you get confirmation from the Hornets that he's on the trading block or not?'; 'Who's covering the diving competition?'

This cacophony made it necessary to conduct most of my interviews 'on the fly' – the organized chaos of a newsroom rarely allows for long interviews. Yet I was fortunate that all the sports newsworkers made an effort to escape the newsroom so that I could conduct more formally structured and lengthy interviews. To this end, I carried a series of questions (an 'interview schedule') in the back of my field diary that I would use as a loose guide (see Appendix).

To initiate an interview, I approached newsworkers in a conversational manner, trying to relate to them on a level of shared affection for sports and sports journalism rather than as a detached social scientist. I found it particularly useful to tell them I had been a varsity football player at one of the local universities for five years. This was a great 'ice-breaker' and led to many interesting conversations, especially with a few of the reporters who had, at various times, covered university football in the city. This approach worked well, and after a short while I was on a first-name basis with all the sports newsworkers at the paper.

Each interview began with an explanation that I was interested in how the sports section of a metropolitan daily newspaper is put together, and in particular that I wanted to know about the interviewee's role in this process. I discussed anonymity and confidentiality, explaining how I would blend their views and opinions in with those of their colleagues, both in the analysis and in the writing. I told them I would illustrate and highlight certain points by using anecdotes from individual interviews, and explained that I would identify individuals with either pseudonyms or by their occupational title (e.g., editor, desker, beat reporter); further, I told them of my intention to disguise the name and location of the newspaper.

I then asked them to tell me about their work, beginning with a general overview of what their jobs mean, what they entail in the daily production of sports news. As these discussions unfolded, I interjected questions along the way, loosely following the interview schedule while at the same time trying to focus the interview. In fact, the interview schedule was used only as a guide, and no attempt was made to restrict the interview subject too much to any one topic. This approach allowed for probing and for following leads provided by the subject. In fact, exploring the channels opened up by respondents offered a wealth of information that likely would not have come to the surface had I strictly adhered to an interview schedule. People were very candid in their responses to sometimes difficult and possibly uncomfortable questions. For example, when asked point-blank why major-league sports receive so much coverage in the paper and others so little – a potentially threatening question – not one respondent avoided making a direct and forthright response. Indeed, they did not hesitate in pointing to the economic logic of such biased coverage: 'Because that's what people want to read about' and 'That's what gets you readers' were typical responses.

I believe this frankness was, in large part, a reflection of their voluntary participation. From the outset, the *Examiner*'s sports newsworkers demonstrated a great deal of enthusiasm for this study, with many going out of their way to ensure I captured as much data as possible. 'You should talk to Bobby Barnes about that,' and 'I really want to read this when you're done' are typical of the support I received. One reporter even gave me his home phone number so I could call him 'any time' I had a question. This enthusiasm and support greatly contributed to the depth of analysis this study was able to achieve.

Scheduled interviews lasted from forty to sixty minutes on average, depending on how busy the newsworker was; spontaneous interviews generally ranged from several minutes to twenty. All interviews were tape-recorded without objection. As a point of interest, several newsworkers seemed amused that they were now the ones being interviewed, sitting on the other side of the fence so to speak; one respondent commented that he 'felt like a jock under the microscope after a big game.'

In addition to the interview data, a lot of empirical material was obtained by making an observation and then approaching a newsworker to ask about it. For example, when I observed a reporter casually stroll over to the fax machine and begin to sift through the faxes that had arrived in the last fifteen minutes I asked him, 'What are they? Get a lot of them?' These two simple questions led to a twenty-minute discussion of press releases and their importance to sports newswork.

3

Working the Sports Beat

The sports pages have consistently told me the sports I participate in don't count as sports, and the sports I like to watch don't count as sports. Editors, writers, producers and advertisers are primarily white, wealthy men. Sports coverage reflects their interests and their attachment to the status quo.

Mariah Burton Nelson, *The Stronger Women Get the More Men Love Football*

News industry economics dictate that metropolitan dailies fill their sports pages almost exclusively with news from the world of major-league sport. Given this reality, the dilemma facing the Big City *Examiner* is how to cover such a vast expanse? After all, daily newspapers, like any news organization, have finite human and financial resources; it is impossible to post reporters everywhere there is a big-ticket event happening. As the *Examiner*'s assistant sports editor put it, 'Obviously we can't have somebody covering a hockey game in Pittsburgh, in Colorado, and in Toronto, you know, on the same night. It just isn't possible for any paper to have that kind of coverage. Can you imagine the size of the staff you'd need and the money it would take to fly them all over the place? It just isn't possible; it would be nice, though.' The answer is to employ a coverage strategy that is an industry standard, and has been for over one hundred years – the 'beat' system of reporting.

The Structural Framework of the Sports Beat

Generally speaking, *beat* coverage consists of assigning a reporter to a particular organization in order to provide regular coverage of a subject. News beats are a way of providing *predictably available information* to reporters and, as such, are an important means of reducing the variability of news, of imposing a degree of order on the social world. In this sense, a news beat constitutes 'the routine round of institutions and persons to be contacted at scheduled intervals for knowledge of events.'[1]

With sports this means assigning a reporter to cover a major sports team in order to provide regular news stories not only about its activities, but also about the sport itself. Take, for example, a big Toronto daily that assigns one of its reporters to the Blue Jays beat. Day in and day out this reporter is supposed to be on top of the team's activities, reporting on anything significant (as we shall see below, *insignificance* also matters) that happens involving the team's ownership, its management, its players and coaches, and, when necessary, its opponents. Beat writers are expected to know their terrain intimately, and write regular news items about its activities. In this manner the newspaper gets regular coverage not only of the Blue Jays, but of Major League Baseball itself. How? Simply because the team does not exist in a vacuum. When the reporter writes about the Blue Jays, invariably this means covering the activities of all the other teams in the major leagues, or at least those with whom the Jays come in contact. The Blue Jays beat, therefore, generates a regular flow of baseball news not only about the team, but about Major League Baseball as a whole.

Moreover, beat reporters must provide extensive coverage of their team *throughout the year*. During the playing season they cover training camp, practices, and games, as well as community events and other such activities. In the off-season, beat reporters also keep a sharp eye on their team, speculating on trades, coaching changes, movement of free agents, and likely top choices in the amateur draft. As one beat reporter put it, 'I spend so much time with these guys it's like I live with them. All year I go on their road trips, I cover their home games, I go to most of their practices, I cover the draft – everything that happens with this team I know about.'

Media scholar Gaye Tuchman has likened this process of capturing news in such a systematic (and ultimately limiting) manner to casting a fishing net.[2] A net's haul depends upon the amount invested in its intersecting fibre and the tensile strength of that fibre: the narrower the intersections between the mesh, the more that can be captured. 'Of course, designing a more expensive narrow mesh presupposes a desire to catch small fish, not a wish to throw them back into the flow of amorphous everyday occurrences.'[3] Today's news net is intended for *big fish*, the big news stories that attract and hold readers' attention over long periods of time, and so the net is full of gaping holes as organizational resources are invested in a highly restricted and strategic fashion. Small fish are of little interest. This is especially the case with sports news.

In casting the sports news net, newspapers aim to capture major-league sporting spectacles – those intense entertainments so useful for marshalling large male audiences. These are the big fish so eagerly sought. The *Examiner*'s sports section is the near-exclusive domain of the major leagues. 'We build the section around the big sports that our readers want to know about,' explained Bob Roberts, the paper's sports editor. Several of his staffers echoed this sentiment when asked why the paper has so much coverage of the CFL, the NBA, and other major-league sports. For example, one remarked: 'We have so much coverage of them obviously because they're big-time sports ... people want to read about them.'

And what of the little fish, how do they fare? Beat reporter Buck Colvin gives a good indication of the general attitude at the paper: 'People want to read about professional sports, the big leagues ... A lot of people don't watch little Billy go play ball at Trillium Park on a Friday night. I mean how much interest is there in sports like that? Not enough to warrant a lot of coverage.' Consequently, coverage of non-commercial sports is sporadic at best; certainly none can boast of receiving the enormous coverage enjoyed by the big leagues. The *Examiner*'s coverage of the local university and college sports scene, for example, is usually assigned to Chet Burkley, a part-time reporter. As he explains, 'We don't have a beat for amateur sports, at least not like we do for the [professional sports teams in the city] ... I mostly cover university sports for the *Examiner*. You know, there isn't a full-timer who does it.'

Sometimes beat reporters will be assigned to cover a non-commercial sports event – but only when they aren't occupied by their regular duties. In short, little regard accrues to non-commercial sports as worthwhile news subjects. Beat reporters (who are, along with columnists, considered a newspaper's best reporters) only cover non-commercial sports when they aren't busy covering a major event. The lack of consideration given non-commercial sports by the *Examiner* is an indication of the paper's economic priorities – these sports simply do not contribute to the bottom line, and thus are given little more than an afterthought on a routine basis.

The *Examiner* employs a beat system to cover the commercial sports scene – to ensure its daily haul of big fish. The paper assigns four reporters on a full-time basis to three different teams: two are assigned to Big City's National Hockey League franchise; one to the Canadian Football League franchise; and one to the Triple 'A' baseball franchise (though periodically these beat assignments do overlap). These organizations function as central nodes of news activity in Big City's sports world, certain to generate the sort of news considered most appealing to male sports fans. These are the 'bread and butter' sports news subjects, and the *Examiner* lavishes its resources on them.

What must be taken into account in this regard is that establishing and maintaining a series of sports beats constitutes a significant investment of organizational resources – beat coverage does not come cheap. The *Examiner*'s sports editor noted that it costs the paper well in excess of $10,000 per year to provide beat coverage of Big City's CFL team. Over and above salary, the paper has to pay for the reporter's transportation on road trips, his hotel accommodation, and per diem money to cover meals and incidentals. And this is only one of three beats. 'Magnify that several times and that's what it costs us to cover [the NHL team]. Because their season's a lot longer than football, you're paying for more road trips, more hotels, meals, all that sort of thing ... plus there is a lot of travel in the U.S., which costs us in the exchange rate.'

The costs of sending a reporter on the road with their team are clearly quite substantial. In the past, professional sports organizations typically covered most of these expenses, or at least contributed a good deal towards. Today, however, teams no longer pick up the tab; media outlets are expected to cover their own costs. The director of media relations for Big City's NHL team, Gaston Rouge, was especially blunt when I asked him about this: 'They pay their own way. We don't fund the media!' As far as he is concerned, 'it's up to them to cover their reporters' expenses. They can make their own travel arrangements or they can do it through us. Either way, they pay for their own airplane tickets and hotels, and to travel on our team bus we bill them $8.00 a head.' This is also the case with the CFL team. As their director of communications explains, 'We'll book them hotel rooms and air fare at our preferred rate, you know, get them a good deal because we get discounts. But no way, we don't pay for it; that's their concern.'

Human resources are another significant cost associated with the beat system of reporting. When a reporter is assigned to cover a major-league sports team as a regular beat, the CFL team for instance, that reporter is the *Examiner*'s full-time CFL reporter. During the CFL season it is his job every day to write stories about the team and, more generally, about activities in the league. As a result, this reporter is mostly unavailable to cover other events, particularly those at the local community level. The impact of this specialization on the *Examiner*'s sports-news content is significant.

Essentially, the beat system limits the number of sports reporters available to cover non-commercial sports events – they are already committed to major commercial sports teams. If the *Examiner*'s three beat reporters are all occupied with their regular responsibilities (covering their respective teams), that leaves only two deskers and one part-timer to cover Big City's non-commercial sports scene. Under these conditions, the opportunity for non-commercial sports to wrestle some news space from the major-league sports teams is minimal, since most of the paper's staff and financial resources are preoccupied with the latter.

Moreover, because only the *Examiner*'s best reporters are assigned to these beats, the argument can be made that the *quality* of non-commercial sports coverage is significantly lower than that afforded to commercial sports. After all, it is unlikely the paper would assign a cub reporter, a stringer, or a reporter with marginal or average skills to cover a major sports beat – the newspaper has far too much invested in these beats to assign any but its best reporters to them.

The *Examiner* commits such significant human and financial resources to its beats for the simple reason that they generate the sort of news integral to producing a quality sports-audience commodity. Jim McDermott, the paper's assistant sports editor, underscored this point when I asked him why the *Examiner* invests so heavily in establishing and maintaining its three sports beats: 'Oh, our beats are indispensable!' He elaborated, noting that the paper has one reporter, Bobby Barnes, assigned full-time to the CFL beat for nearly two hundred days a year: 'This is to [ensure] we've always got stuff on the team. Even in the off-season he's always digging up [CFL] stuff ... He's basically our full-time CFL reporter.' Thus, Barnes is responsible for everything that happens with the team: 'It's his club and he's got to maintain contact with it, be aware of every development, both major and minor.' The rationale for this is straightforward: 'You've got to have beat guys always know what's happening with their team. They have to follow their team at all times because it's the only way they can stay on top of what's going on. And your readers want to know what's happening with [the big leagues], you know, that's where the public interest is. They want to know about professional sports. It's that simple.' Clearly, the *Examiner* depends on its major-league sports beats to produce regular flows of commercial sports news. As far as the paper's sportswriters and editors are concerned, beats are fountains of raw news material meant for conversion into news appealing primarily to male sports fans. This is precisely why daily newspapers like the *Examiner* invest so heavily in establishing and maintaining major-league sports beats.

In short, the costs of employing a beat system of reporting are considerable. The range of coverage in the sports section is constrained by limitations of space and staff. It follows that those teams that are the subjects of a beat will be featured in the paper on a daily basis – it is they that receive regular and extensive coverage in the most prominent pages of the sports section.

It is not surprising, then, that the *Examiner* fills its sports pages each day with news generated from its three commercial sports beats. Accordingly, non-commercial sports often find themselves buried in the back pages when they do manage to get some coverage. Why else would a newspaper make such a substantial investment of organizational resources to establish and maintain major-league sports beats, if not to rely on them to produce the bulk of the news with which it intends to fill the sports section?

Working the Sports Beat

The *Examiner* utilizes a system of beats to generate nearly all its sports news, which amounts to a huge draw on organizational resources, both human and financial. The expected return on this investment is lots of fresh copy daily from these. Indeed, the *Examiner*'s assignment of beat reporters to only three professional sports teams is strong evidence of its commitment to providing extensive coverage of major-league sports. As we've already seen, this is for the purpose of manufacturing a quality male-audience commodity, one that is highly concentrated and clearly defined and thus appealing to advertisers.

What we need to do now, in light of this background on the 'structural framework' of the sports beat, is turn our attention to the *Examiner*'s sportswriters and their daily work routines on the beat. In particular, we need to gain a better understanding of the paper's sports newswork environment and the production practices that constitute it, identifying the specific pressures and constraints under which sportswriters do their work.

Filling the Sports Newshole

Just how much sports news reporters must produce from their beats varies, depending primarily on the amount of space available on a given day – what is called the 'newshole.' The size of the newshole also varies, depending on the amount of advertising space the paper has sold for that day. Quite simply, 'news space is driven by ad revenue.' As Sam Snead, one of the *Examiner*'s deskers, explains: 'The size of the sports section varies every day. It all depends on advertising – that's what everything in the paper depends on. The number of ads you sell determines how big the paper will be; you can't have a 100-page paper with only three ads in it because you're going to lose a lot of money real fast. Ads determine news space – that's the key. Our advertising people often joke that they take care of my pay cheque and, really, that's more or less the case.' Sports editor Bob Roberts elaborates on the importance of advertising sales, not only to the paper's financial bottom line but also in determining the size the sports section: 'The amount of space we have each day is dictated solely by the amount of advertising we have.' What this means is that 'advertising has to remain at a certain level to pay all the bills. If there's a lot of advertising the paper gets bigger and there's a lot more space for sports.'

As a point of illustration, when I was conducting my interview with Sam Snead we were interrupted by a phone call from Pete Dewey, the paper's Triple 'A' baseball beat reporter. He was calling from Scranton, Ohio, just before the team's game that evening, to ask how long his story had to be. Snead told him, 'I wouldn't write nine inches or anything like that. We've only got four pages today.' Questioned about this reply, Snead explained that because it was a Monday, a day when advertising sales are typically down, the sports section is allotted minimal space compared to other days: 'A lot of it has to do with the fact that advertisers don't want to spend money advertising on days when readership is down. You'll notice that most papers are bigger later in the week because everything is geared for the weekend shopper ... People get paid on Thursday, for instance, so they've got money to spend, and that's when advertisers want to reach them, by placing ads in our paper.' What we find here is that advertising concerns largely determine not only the *content* of sports news – there is a profound major-league sports bias in the *Examiner* because this is perceived to be the sort of sports news that attracts a predominantly male readership – but also the *amount* of news content in each edition. The more advertising space purchased, the more space there is for major-league sports news, generally speaking.

Story Quotas

Examiner reporters are expected to fill the paper's sports pages with major-league sports news every day. There are no hard and fast rules regarding how many items are to be produced; as noted above, the size of the sports newshole varies. 'Some days they write one story, others five or six,' explained one editor. 'But there's no set quota carved in stone. I don't tell so-and-so that every Tuesday he's gotta give me four stories on whatever. It depends on how much is happening on his beat and how much space I've got to fill.'

What *is* cast in stone, though, is the obligation for reporters to write *something* about their beat every day. This is not negotiable – the newspaper has too much invested in its sports beats for them to sit idle. The *Examiner*'s sports editor puts this point into context, noting that 'it costs us a hell of a lot of money to maintain a beat ... so you bet they'd better produce! We spend a lot of money to have these guys know what's going on with their team and to write about it.' I asked one of the deskers what would happen to a reporter who wasn't producing enough news items from their beat. His reply is telling: 'He won't have his job for very long.'

Covering a sports beat thus entails an obligation to write every day about its activities, about both the team and the general 'goings-on' of the league. This obligation is so strong that reporters are expected to produce stories even if they don't think there is anything really newsworthy to report. The guiding principle is that no matter what, there is *always* something to report, 'whether it's the previous night's game, a trade rumour, [or] maybe someone isn't playing well and they've been benched or they're hurt.' As far as the *Examiner*'s sports editor is concerned, this is necessary even if it's a 'slow news day,' when nothing much of significance is going on. In this instance, 'feature stories are always good, like the rookie who's having a great season so far, or maybe one of the players has an interesting hobby or something like that ... People like to read human-interest stories.' Whatever the case may be, the sports editor was emphatic that his reporters have to be continually producing news.

But what if a reporter decides not to submit any news items about his beat because there is simply nothing worth writing about? To the paper's sports editor this is unconscionable: 'Oh, he'll find something, he has too. As I told you, that's what they're paid for – writing stories about their team. Besides, between practices and games our guys spend so much time with their teams that they can't help but come up with something.' This point, that reporters must generate fresh copy from their beats daily *whether or not there is anything really newsworthy to report*, was made in one way or another by all the newsworkers interviewed. Here is the assistant sports editor, who explains matter-of-factly that there is always a story to write: 'You know, it may be a slow news day but they can contact their sources and dig something up. Sometimes what they come up with isn't that great, but it's still a story.'

What these comments from the *Examiner*'s editorial staff underscore is how the paper's coverage strategy – designed and implemented to capture a regular supply of major-league sports news – puts an incredible amount of pressure on reporters to constantly produce fresh copy from their beats, no matter what. In effect, the *Examiner*'s sports editors view each of their beats as (to borrow from media theorist Mark Fishman) a 'bottomless pit where one can always find something to write about.'[4] And they expect their reporters to regard those beats in the same manner.

I questioned part-time reporter Chet Burkley about this issue. He complained that 'there's a lot of pressure on us to write stories, even if nothing is really going on.' Every single day reporters are forced to come up with something, even if its the most banal story imaginable: 'To me, that's bullshit,' declared Burkley. Take beat writer Buck Colvin, for example: 'Buck has to come up with something on [the NHL team] every day of the season, and even in the off-season. He's got to stay on top of everything that's happening with them, you know, trades and all that ... So you get a lot of player profile stories, stories about the big rivalry between the home team and their arch rivals coming up in a few days. Stuff like that you've got to make a big deal about when it's slow on your beat.' Lack of activity on a sports beat is thus insufficient grounds for a reporter not to generate news. As Fishman notes, 'The sense of how little or how much is happening is largely irrelevant to the normative requirement for reporters to produce these stories.'[5]

The journalistic aphorism 'no news is news' is a convention at the *Examiner*, and likely at all metropolitan daily newspapers utilizing the beat system of reporting – there's always something on the beat to write about, even if it's 'bullshit.' However, as former sports editor Leonard Shecter wryly observes, 'if a daily newspaper were to be really honest it would, on many days, not appear at all on the reasonable ground that there was no news today.'[6]

In short, the whole point of the reporter's beat work is to generate major-league sports news to fill the sports section. The sense of how little or how much is actually happening is largely irrelevant to the normative requirement – without exception – for reporters to produce these stories.

Deadlines

Compounding the pressure on journalists of having to generate varying quantities of news from their beats every day is the problem of doing so under relentless and inflexible deadlines beyond their control. Reporters must schedule their information-gathering routines and writing activity around the daily production schedule of the newspaper. Indeed, it is imperative that sportswriters file their stories on time, since each stage of production depends upon completion of an earlier stage; the actual writing of sports copy is only the first stage. Once submitted, all copy has to be vetted, accompanying photos selected and cropped, headlines composed, pages laid out, and final approval from the editor received before the sports section is ready for incorporation into that day's edition of the paper and the paper itself goes to press.

At the *Examiner* all copy is to be submitted to the sports desk no later than 11:00 p.m. As Jim McDermott, the paper's assistant sports editor explains, 'We have to have the first edition cleared and off the floor, ready to go to press by 11:15 p.m. This means that all the pages have to be laid out, and camera-ready, ready to be shot by the camera which turns it into newsprint ... All this has to be done by 11:15 or so in order to get the first edition done. It's the first edition of the paper which serves the outlying areas. The final edition has to be done for 1:00 a.m., so they've got to get their stories in by 11:00 p.m. and no later!' Given these strict temporal restraints on the production process, there is almost a militant enforcement of deadline. Little quarter is given a reporter failing to submit copy, as McDermott makes strikingly clear: 'They have to! Being late is not an option! And believe me, they'll hear about it when they don't meet a deadline. We've got two editions a night, and if they don't meet the first one, they'd bloody well better have the story ready for the second. I mean, if they miss the first edition, they miss half our readership.'

One of the *Examiner*'s beat reporters echoed this point when I asked him point-blank what happens if a reporter repeatedly fails to get his copy in on time. He looked at me incredulously and exclaimed: 'You've got to! You've got to meet the deadline. If you don't then you won't have a job tomorrow.'

Clearly the obligation to meet deadline, like the obligation to generate fresh news copy every day, is a normative requirement of working a sports beat for the *Examiner*. All the sports news-workers I interviewed were emphatic in their insistence that deadlines are inviolable. As one reporter put it, meeting dead-line is one of the 'Golden Rules' of sports journalism.

The game story, unlike the feature or personal profile type of news item, is a mix of description, quotation, and analysis. The key to writing good game stories is exercising judgment about what is newsworthy: Was one team in control from the start? Did they blow their lead in the closing minutes? Did a star player have an exceptionally poor performance? Maybe a rookie or third-stringer (even a wily old veteran whose career was thought to be all but over) came off the bench and shone, while the big-bucks players were lackadaisical. Did a single error make the dif-ference in the outcome? These are the signposts sportswriters are looking for. As *Globe and Mail* sports columnist Stephen Brunt says, 'You have to figure out the key moment, or the turn-ing point or the story within the game ... Then you go and talk to the people involved, and write it from that perspective.'[7]

The problem for sportswriters, though, is that the critical judgment about the key moment of the game has to be made in a matter of minutes, sometimes as the reporter is heading to the clubhouse for post-game interviews. So the amount of scoring play and other such factual material that actually goes into a story depends primarily on how close the reporter is to deadline. Alison Gordon, former baseball writer for the *Toronto Star*, notes that game stories are very difficult in professional sports pre-cisely because of the need to beat deadline. Night-time Blue Jays games usually ended at the same time as her first deadline at the *Star*, so she wrote while watching the game: 'You write down the scoring – "White singled, stole second, went to third on so-and-so's infield hit and scored on Carter's double" – that kind of bor-ing stuff ... But you do that to fill space. Then, when you find your angle, your lead, you write very fast and file for the early edition.'[8] Once these basic elements of the game story are cov-ered, 'you race down to the clubhouse, get your quotes, race back up and rewrite the story for the later edition. At that point, you're dumping a lot of that scoring-play stuff.'

The important point to note here is the problem of covering a beat where events typically finish only a short time before deadline. With the Big City *Examiner* and its filing deadline of 11:00 p.m. for sports stories, this time frame creates problems for reporters since night games (the time most major-league sports events are held) normally don't end until 10:30 p.m.

Pete Dewey offers a good illustration of how deadline pressures affect his work on the Triple 'A' baseball beat. During the first year he covered the team (which was also the club's first year of existence) all evening games where scheduled for a 7:30 p.m. start. With games often going a full three-hour stretch, and the *Examiner*'s 11:00 p.m. deadline looming, Dewey found himself constantly 'working against the clock':

Here at the *Examiner* [the deadline is] eleven o'clock, which is kind of tough to meet a lot of the time when you're doing a night game. During the first year for the team, the games didn't start until 7:30 and they weren't getting over until a half-hour or so before deadline ... So it makes it a real challenge to get your [stories] written – I've got to cover the basics of the game, who scored when, big plays, all that. Then I've got to do my interviews, get my quotes. And after all that I've got to finish writing my stories. But when there's only a half-hour or less before deadline, it can get [harried].

Just how great an impact the deadline has on beat work routines is further demonstrated by Dewey. He goes on to explain that the pressure of beating deadline wasn't so bad the second year he covered the baseball team because the starting time for night games had been moved up by a half-hour, buying him that much more time to write his post-game stories: 'I get a little bit of leeway now. So now I can go down to the clubhouse and talk to the players and actually kind of think about what I'm going to write. [The extra time] just makes things a bit easier.'

This relentless pressure to beat deadline means that sportswriters often only 'see about half the events they're attending, often stuffing conditional leads into they're computers – if this team wins use this one and if that team wins use that one, occasionally glancing up from the machine to see how the game's progressing.'[9]

Sportswriters must arrange their workday around the newspaper's deadlines – even though their beat work is focused on a domain of activities that usually pays no heed to these deadlines. So no matter where they are on their beat or what they're doing, the *Examiner*'s fixed deadlines require sports reporters to allocate their time strategically and efficiently and arrange their schedules so they can have their copy in on time. As Leonard Koppett puts it: 'The most brilliant piece of writing in the history of mankind is worthless, to the newspaper, if it misses the deadline. And the most rudimentary information – 'Red Sox win,' for instance – is of considerable value if it beats the deadline and gets into print.'[10]

4

The Routine Sources of Sports News

We're not in this business to establish friendships with sources. We're in it to establish *relationships*.

Sportswriter Buck Colvin

The *Examiner*'s newswork environment is shot through with pressures and constraints. Every day the paper expects its sportswriters to cover all the ground their beat territory encompasses, and to continuously produce news of the major-league sports world under imposing and rigid deadlines. As we shall see in this chapter, the only way reporters can possible satisfy these demands is by strategically and systematically exposing themselves to a limited number of routine news sources. In other words, *Examiner* sportswriters need sources whom they can count on to provide a steady flow of news material all the time; that these routine sources are a reporter's 'lifeblood' is a common metaphor used to describe their significance.

Who are these routine sources? The obvious ones that leap to mind are athletes, coaches, and management types; not so obvious sources are player agents, team doctors and trainers, equipment managers, front-office administrative staff, and even other sports reporters to a limited degree. For analytical purposes, I have established two general categories of routine sources: (1) major-league sports organizations and their more senior staff, and (2) personal contacts on the beat.

Both groupings constitute routine sources for *Examiner* sportswriters because they satisfy the reporters' need for continuous flows of fresh news material every day. Significantly, both source types are representatives of the major-league sports world; and because reporters generally limit themselves to these sources, coverage in the daily press privileges these sports. Sports news is about them.

1. Major-League Sports Organizations

Big-time sports organizations are only too happy to offer their services to media outlets and their reporters. Knowing the nature of sportswriters' dependence on them for raw news material, major-league sports teams and leagues have, over several decades, learned to cater to the practical concerns of journalists in order to serve their own promotional needs. As this chapter will show, commercial sports organizations go to great trouble and expense to facilitate sports newswork – to make it easier for reporters to do their job.

Through their media-relations staff in particular, sports organizations provide a steady stream of news material in the form of press releases and news conferences. They also provide a whole raft of services and facilities at event venues that help sportswriters to cope with the exigencies of their work. The payoff for these efforts is ubiquitous and prominent presence in the daily sports news; in other words, invaluable publicity in the form of media coverage – what amounts to 'publicity-as-news.' The upshot of all this is that major-league sports organizations are able to effect a measure of control over what becomes sports news and how it is reported.

Media Relations Staffers

The corporate offices of big-time sports organizations all have in-house media relations units, staffed with experts whose primary function is to meet the information needs of journalists. Gaston Rouge, director of media relations for Big City's NHL team, characterized his job as being that of a 'facilitator,' an information manager. As he sees it, media relations is all about the controlled 'dissemination of information' in accord with the promotional interests of the team. 'From our point of view, as a professional sports organization, it's a matter of how to best disseminate your information in order to, well, let's be fair: you have to maximize the coverage of your team, and the best way to do that is [to] help the journalists do their job.' The director of communications for the Big City CFL team articulates his role in a similar fashion, likening himself to a football quarterback (a 'field general' in sports parlance). 'My job is to facilitate theirs, to make sure they have everything available to them,' he explains. 'I'm like a quarterback, you know, my job is to disseminate ideas and to get our word out to reporters, and to make our personnel accessible in order to make their job easier.' Both of these media relations staffers characterized the purpose of media relations as *facilitating newswork*, as providing reporters with *efficient service*. This service is crucial to securing enormous amounts of daily media coverage, or as Rouge put it, to 'getting lots and lots of ink.'

In this respect it is common for commercial sports organizations to staff their media relations units with people who have an in-depth knowledge of the journalism craft. These are primarily people who understand what sports newswork is all about: people who know what constitutes a newsworthy event; what the pressures and constraints of newswork are in terms of story quotas and deadlines; when to hold a press conference; what information to put in a press release; what facilities, services, and equipment reporters need at event venues (such as electrical outlets, phone jacks for modems, television monitors, and telephones).

In other words, media relations people must understand *media logic* and *media formats* to facilitate sports newswork. As one staffer puts it, 'You've got to know as much about them [reporters] as you can ... what their job is all about and how they do it. That's the key to doing this job.' Armed with such 'recipe knowledge,'[1] media relations workers are able to facilitate newswork much more effectively.

In his classic 1955 study of sports promotion, Canadian sociologist Bruce McFarlane found that promoters recruit their media relations staff (he uses the classical term 'press agent') almost exclusively from the ranks of sports reporters. Of the twenty press agents employed by the larger sports promotion interests in the major Canadian city he studied, sixteen were ex-sportswriters or were currently employed on a full-time basis in a newspaper office. McFarlane observes that the press agent's sportswriting experience is largely responsible for clearing a path from the newsroom to media relations work. First, agents know the type of material sportswriters are interested in, that is, what is 'newsworthy.' Second, they know the extent to which the sportswriter's job is controlled by rigid time deadlines. And third, they have developed a wide circle of friends and acquaintances among sportswriters because of their on-the-job associations with them.[2] Overall, McFarlane's findings underscore the importance of understanding the nature of newswork and newswork routines to the objective of attaining media coverage.

I don't want to make too much of the need for prior journalistic experience to doing good media relations work. Obviously there's a case to be made for media relations training programs in colleges and universities (some schools offer specific degree and certificate programs in sports administration). But I do want to emphasize that possessing a thorough understanding of sports journalism and all it entails is key to obtaining media coverage. And this requires that media relations staffers understand all facets of sports newswork – from concerns surrounding newsgathering to the temporal constraints that affect and ultimately control sports newswork.

So it follows that what makes experienced reporters so attractive to major-league sports organizations is their practical work experience – the wide circle of personal contacts in the media they've developed over the years, as well as the 'news sense' and knowledge of the reporter's job that one obtains first-hand while working as a sports reporter. As one sports editor told McFarlane: 'I think that the best place for a man to become a publicity man is to get out and work for a newspaper for some time ... because that's where he gets to meet a lot of contacts.

These contacts are very, very good because he gets to know how to handle deadlines, things like that ... [Sports organizations] like to have ex-newspaper men, fellows who have all the contacts, who know all the people in sports.'[3] These basic tenets of sports promotional work have changed little in the more than forty years since McFarlane did this pioneering work.

Many of the basic principles McFarlane identified remain at the core of contemporary media relations work in the sports entertainment industry. For instance, I asked Gaston Rouge to explain how necessary it was for him to have working experience as a journalist in order to do good media relations work in this industry. 'It's important to know what sports journalists want, and this is where my background in journalism and PR helps ... It helps if you've been on 'the other side of the fence,' because you understand how [reporters] work, how they like their information packaged. By "packaged" I mean how reporters like their news releases printed, when they want press conferences scheduled ... Really, it's all about knowing how to make a big deal out of something that isn't, and how to target an event specifically for television as opposed to radio or print.' For media relations staffers to facilitate sports newswork, they must have a thorough understanding *how to package information* in such a fashion that it is going to find its way into a news story or, as is often the case, into several news stories.

In the same vein, the CFL team's director of communications argues that media relations work in the professional sports industry is 'more of an operations thing.' By this he means that having a thorough understanding of what sports journalism entails is key to being able to meet reporters' needs. 'Well, literally, I mean knowing how sports journalists operate, how they do their job and what they need to do it. The more you know about them, then the better able you are to facilitate their work.' For example, he elaborates that it is incumbent on him to know the various deadlines all the different reporters work under. Different newspaper organizations have different deadlines, as do Big City's various radio and television stations: 'I have to know the deadlines that all the journalists work under. They're all different, you know, beat reporters from the papers run on a totally different schedule from the TV and radio guys. If you know this – and you *have* to know this – you know when to hold your press conferences, you know what equipment they need in the press box or whatever.' Another veteran sportswriter takes this view, that an intimate familiarity with reporters' needs is the key to doing sports media relations work. He knows several people who have left sports journalism to get into media relations work, hoping to capitalize on their working knowledge of journalism by 'working for the other team,' as he puts it metaphorically. 'Professional sports organizations that hire ex-reporters to do their PR are really smart because they know exactly what reporters want,' he explains. 'Tennis Canada has a PR guy who used to cover the Blue Jays for Canadian Press. [Based on this experience] he knows what is newsworthy, what reporters need to write a story.'

The intimate knowledge of sports newswork that former reporters bring with them to media relations work is extremely useful. Armed with such *recipe knowledge*, media relations staffers are better equipped to facilitate sports newswork – and are thus better able to advance their organization's promotional interests. Smart media relations people know exactly what the deadline times are for all the major media in their immediate market, and are sure to orient their daily promotional activities to correspond to them.

Press conferences, for example, are scheduled to correspond with media deadlines. If they deviate even slightly, 'there's going to be hell to pay,' explains one media relations director: 'Imagine calling Brock Smith [a local sports anchor] at 5:00 p.m. and telling him we're having a big news conference at 5:30 p.m. He'd be screaming "What the hell are you thinking! You're calling me now when my line-up of stories for the night is already done. What are you doing, breaking this story when I'm on the air in an hour-and-a-half!" There's no way they could get a crew in to cover the conference and have the piece ready [for air by 7:00 p.m.]. You see? That's why you've got to know how the media people work.' It is therefore vital that major media events such as news conferences are scheduled in accord with the production schedules of news organizations. 'You can't have a conference at 5:30 p.m. because the TV guys can't come; and the press guys, they want it in the early afternoon so they can contact their sources, maybe get an inside angle on the story or something like that.'

The pursuit of wide coverage demands that media relations people pay strict attention to the deadlines of all news organizations, regardless of medium. The post-game period offers an excellent illustration of this necessity. Immediately following the end of an event, sportswriters have to hustle to the locker rooms to do their interviews with athletes and coaches. Time is of the essence here, because games usually end with minimal time to spare before deadline; and once they have got their quotes, sportswriters still need time to finish rewriting their news items and get them submitted in time for final copy-editing, headlining, and layout. After a game, though, most teams have a closed-door policy designed to give the coaching staff time alone with their team. With production deadlines looming, it is up to the media relations people to make sure that coaches keep 'No Press Time' on schedule (usually about fifteen minutes) and, subsequently, that reporters have unimpeded access to the locker room to get their quotes.

Jimmy Jones, the CFL team's director of communications, explains that as a media relations staffer working a big-ticket sports event, 'you're never more aware of deadlines than post-game':

After a home game we have fifteen minutes to keep the locker room closed; but after that we open it to the media so they can go in and talk to the coach, talk to the players, do their interviews and that sort of thing. Your beat reporters, they have to file their stories by, say, 11:00 p.m., and they have to get their quotes. So my job is to make sure everyone can get in and get their stuff and get out as quick as possible. And they're pretty bitter if they can't do it because they get heat from their editor if they don't get their stories in on time.

Notice that in order to facilitate sports newswork after the game by ensuring reporters 'get their quotes' so they can 'have their stories in on time,' it is crucial that media relations people know the production deadlines reporters face. This may seem a small point – but it's essential to recognize that time is a precious commodity for sportswriters; none can be wasted if they are to beat deadline.

Summing up thus far – the media relations function in major-league sport is almost exclusively devoted to *servicing the media* in the following ways:

- Issuing regular press releases and scheduling news conferences to notify sports reporters of potentially newsworthy events.
- Setting up and operating a comfortable working area for the press, with good sight lines of the playing arena, table space, phones, plenty of phone jacks and electrical outlets to accommodate faxes, modems, and laptop computers, good lighting, and protection from rain and wind in the case of outdoor press boxes.
- Arranging for and distributing credentials that give sportswriters, photographers, and broadcasters access to press box, playing field, and clubhouse.
- Writing and distributing Media Guides, which supply factual information in the form of player biographies, statistics, notable achievements, and records. These are invaluable – reporters don't have to waste precious interview time gathering this sort of background material.
- Answering questions as they arise, and communicating with players, officials, and others during a game for on-the-spot clarification of injuries, controversial plays or even line-up changes, and so on.[4]

All this support is provided by major-league sports organizations in their pursuit of obtaining enormous amounts of regular media coverage – the coveted publicity-as-news.

Facilitating Sports Newswork

Working a sports beat is a twenty-four-hour-a-day proposition, but it just is not reasonable to call the coach or general manager or athletes on the hour every hour to ask if anything newsworthy is happening. As Leon Sigal puts it, reporters 'cannot depend on legwork alone to satisfy [their] paper's insatiable demand for news.'[5] Journalists rely on media relations departments to let them know when anything important happens (a trade, an injury status report on a star player, a schedule change) so that they can go about their real task of learning all they can about their beat and reporting on it.

This reality of newswork is used as a 'source tactic,' with media relations staff attempting to 'tie in' reporters to their own promotional agendas by doing much of the legwork for them; for example, providing elaborate 'press kits' with plenty of photographs and background facts and figures that could be useful in writing a sports news item. Given inflexible deadlines, newsworkers 'cannot resist the preformed, prescheduled, and factually safe raw materials that [organizations] provide [through their media relations units].'[6]

Of all the raw materials that sources provide and reporters routinely rely on, no others compare with the *press release* and the *news conference*. Both are channels through which source organizations pass on potentially newsworthy information to reporters – in effect offering them ideas and much of the raw materials they need to write stories.

Press Releases
The press release is a simple device whereby sources notify newsworkers of current or upcoming newsworthy events. Often referred to as 'press kits' or 'knowledge packages,' releases typically contain a detailed account of the event – dates and times, lots of background information including primary facts, and 'quotable quotes' from source representatives.

When crafting a press release, the most important things for media relations staff to keep in mind are the 'five Ws' of writing a news story: Who, What, Where, When, Why. In other words, as one media relations staffer explained, the key is to 'know what basic information reporters need to write a story – and give it to them.' Thus, 'you don't have to be a great writer, as long as you can give [reporters] the basic information so they can determine, "Okay, is there a story here, yes or no? If yes, what is it and how will I treat it as a reporter?"'

From the journalists' perspective, press releases are vital because they provide concise summaries of an event and are rich with factual detail, including the names of key persons to contact for more information and to arrange interviews. Releases also provide extensive background data on athletes; for example, basic biographical material, including age, home town, college/university alma mater, and significant sporting achievements – all this material is precisely what reporters need to write their stories. 'It means we have all this information at our fingertips.' Given the precious little time they have for news-gathering and writing, reporters depend on releases for the basic facts that underlie their news items. 'Public relations people help us a lot. For example, the [NHL team] might provide you with information on [names the team's rookie sensation], you know, he's scored a goal in his last ten straight games or whatever. That's information right there that is very useful. Plus all his past statistics and career highlights are important to know. You get all this kind of information from press releases.'

Press releases, then, offer reporters *pre-packaged news material*. What is more, not only are releases sources of factual detail pertaining to a specific event, organization, or individual, they also function to suggest potentially newsworthy events that news-workers might be unaware of, yet may be interested in covering.

The NHL team's director of media relations underscores this point. He explains that a major part of his job is to offer story ideas to reporters and to provide them with the material they need to write them: 'I'm here to help them do their jobs. It's simply having to know what they want to know. For example, today we signed [names a well-known forward]. First thing I did was prepare a complete news release and send it out to the media.'

This was a 'standard' full-page release. In addition to notifying the media about the news conference scheduled for later that day to announce the signing publicly, the release provided a blurb announcing the acquisition and was replete details about the player's hockey career and 'quotable quotes' from the team's coach and general manager.

With news releases, media relations people are deliberately exploiting sports reporters' need for story ideas and raw news material; in return they expect media coverage of their particular issue, event, or personality. Of course there is no guarantee that a release will be picked up for coverage – the relationship between major-league sports and the media is not of the simple 'stimulus-response' type. The director of media relations for the NHL team explains this point: 'I'll send out a press release to all the local sports media and it's their decision to cover it. All I can do is let them know about something. What I do is let them know this is something they might want to cover, or might have to cover. And they'll decide if there's a story there.'

Even if they don't pick up on a particular press release, it is still a real benefit for reporters to have media relations people 'pitching ideas and stories' at them – especially on a slow news day, when the sports staff may be scrambling to come up with story ideas. A good example of this aspect of suggesting potential news stories is recounted by a media relations staffer with the CFL team: 'A little while ago a lot of our staff and a few of the players went out door-to-door for the Salvation Army and we raised $4000. I thought that was a newsworthy piece. I put out a press release on it because I thought it was good to show people we were out in the community doing stuff. It didn't get picked up by anyone. But it depends, if it's a big news day and there's a lot of other stories in the newspaper, it happens – the story won't get picked up. But if it's a slow news day, it'll probably get picked up.' All this is interesting in light of a major theme running through much of literature on sports reporter-source relations – that it is common practice for press releases to find their way into the sports pages as legitimate news items. In other words, press releases are presented as bona fide news items, as the products of a reporter's legitimate journalistic efforts – when in fact the news items are simply press releases that have been rewritten.

Bruce McFarlane concluded his study of the sociology of sports promotion with the observation that the newsgathering powers of sports journalists were 'emasculated' to the point where they performed simply as 're-write men' – reduced to writing most of their news stories from the contents of press releases issued by promoters rather than 'digging up' news on their own. Consequently, the sports journalists he studied functioned as little more than 'shills' for sports promoters.[7] Dick Beddoes, a noted Canadian sportswriter, echoes these sentiments when he writes: 'There isn't any doubt that sportswriters are bombarded by lobbyists for promotions and often take the easy way out, i.e., they ... accept too many publicity releases as pure gospel.'[8] Garry Smith concurs, arguing that the unqualified acceptance of the information contained in a press release is 'detrimental to the public interest,' as the sports journalist ends up serving the interests of the sports promoter.[9]

The sportswriters I observed, however, emphatically denied that this sort of thing occured to any great extent at the *Examiner* or at any other paper of which they were aware. When asked about the extent of press release rewriting, one reporter explained that 'press releases don't get printed verbatim, no way, never ... I try not to use quotes from them, either.' Another was more direct on the matter, observing that sportswriters 'get a lot of good information from some releases, but you never write them up as a story!' I asked him to explain why, if there's so much useful information in a press release, reporters hesitate to simply rewrite them. 'When it comes down to it, I just don't trust them':

Press release are good for the background stuff, like stats and that sort of thing. But I never use a quote from them because they're generally made up by the PR guy, and just read by the general manager or whoever the quote is attributed to, and he'll just say 'Fine, use it.' Plus, if we did use them, everybody would have the same quotes and, really, you want your own stuff ... Besides, press releases never answer the questions, so you've always got to phone them up and ask questions, check your sources to see what their take on it is.

These assertions by sportswriters that, irrespective of past practice, they don't simply rewrite press releases as genuine news items are corroborated by the NHL team's media relations director. As he explains, this sort of thing is commonplace for minor news items but not for anything significant: 'Well it happens for the little stuff ... We sign a kid from the minors and we have to put a good quote down from [the team's general manager] and a quote from the kid we signed. So, I'll write a release that says something like, Today we signed so-and-so and this is what the GM and coach say, and this kid basically is really happy to be with us. But you're not going to have a major article written by me and sent on official letterhead, published in the paper – that would never happen.'[10] Whether or not sportswriters act as 'reporters' or 'rewrite men,' the most important thing to note about press releases – from the sportswriters' perspective – is that they provide a great deal of information (both useful and useless) that has the effect of making it easier to generate copy every day. This is especially the case on slow news days, when little of significance is happening but something has to be written. The avalanche of press releases burying the *Examiner's* sports desk daily is a gold mine of potential news items.

Press releases, then, are an aspect of promotional work in the major-league sports industry – part and parcel of the incessant efforts of these businesses to secure regular and extensive media coverage of their activities.

News Conferences

News conferences are prescheduled news events that have a function similar to press releases: they provide reporters with a wealth of sports news material. The primary reason for the prima facie news value of conferences lies in the fact that they're held only to announce a significant event. Media relations director Gaston Rouge explains: 'We won't have a news conference unless there's something absolutely new and it looks like there's a lot of questions that are likely to be asked about it. But it would have to be about some new program or major player signing. You know, if we sign a new player and the player isn't in town, why have a news conference? But if he's in town and he's a big name, then for sure we'll call a conference.' The CFL team's director of communications, Jimmy Jones, also stresses the status of news conferences as major events: 'If we draft or trade for a player named John Smith and we think he's going to be a big player for us, and we just put out a press release, it's not going to be as big a deal as if we have a press conference – [the media] pay more attention to us when we hold a conference. If we have a major news conference, with everybody down there [team officials and star players], then that's a major news story and this guy is all of a sudden something special and the media wants to know why.'

As Jones implies, press releases don't command the same attention as do conferences. Accordingly, the news material that releases offer is not always newsworthy. When I asked one editor about this matter, he explained that 'most of the releases we get are useless, you know, we only seriously look at maybe 10 to 20 per cent of the releases that come in, and only a few of those make it into the paper.' In short, if sources can't make a big deal out of an event, rarely will they call a conference. Thus, the special nature of the news conference, as a channel through which reporters can expect especially newsworthy material to flow.

The process and philosophy behind holding a news conference is quite straightforward, and was explained to me by a media-relations staffer with several years' experience. First of all, a 'media advisory' is written and faxed to sports journalists one day in advance of the conference, 'just to let them know about the event, maybe give them some background about what it's going to be about.' These advisories are followed up with a phone call to as many reporters as possible, especially prominent ones, 'just to remind them about the conference, to sort of whet their appetites.' As far as the actual news conference is concerned, the organization makes sure to have 'everyone there who matters': 'Depending on what the conference is all about, we make sure the coach and player or players involved are there to make a statement and answer the media's questions. If it's really important, we'll get the team president or general manager to be there so they can do interviews and answer questions; having big shots like them at the conference lets the media know it's a big deal.' Since 'everyone who matters' is in attendance, the news conference constitutes a rich news source for sports reporters.

News conferences facilitate sports newswork by enabling reporters to collect a lot of news material at one location in a brief period of time. By tapping into this rich news source, sports reporters often access enough information to generate one and sometimes several news items. As reporter Chet Burkley explains:

When you go to a conference, it's usually a pretty big deal, so you do a story about the conference, you know, what the whole thing was about generally. But you also get spin-off stuff where you pick one aspect of the conference and do a [story] on it. For example, say a team calls a conference to announce they've signed a big-name player; you'll write a story about that. But maybe the guy left behind his family [in another city or country]; that's newsworthy. What I mean is, there's always more to write about than the big story; there's always something else.

News conferences organized by major commercial sports organizations, along with press releases, are vitally important promotional tools. They provide reporters with a wealth of easily accessible and newsworthy material that moves them one step closer to fulfilling their daily obligation to generate major-league sports news; at the same time, they help sports teams and organizations advance their own promotional interests.

Other Services

In addition to press releases and news conferences, major-league sports organizations facilitate sports newswork by providing facilities and services at event venues and their corporate offices. Vancouver's General Motors Place is the archetypal modern sports stadium. 'The building was designed with all the modern conveniences to enable to media to do their jobs at the highest level,' explains the media relations director for General Motors Place and the NBA Vancouver Grizzlies (incidentally, he is also a former sports reporter).[11] Unlike the old Pacific Coliseum – where the lighting was poor, seats for reporters were limited, and replay monitors 'were at a premium' – General Motors Place seems like 'the Taj Mahal by comparison.'

The hockey press box at GM Place overhangs the upper deck on the south side just twenty-five metres above ice level, affording reporters an excellent view of the ice. The box seats 154 reporters and broadcasters – up from the Coliseum's 60 – and each seat is equipped with an electrical outlet, data line for modems and fax machines, and a telephone jack. What's more, there are adjustable chairs 'so the lanky and the little can find their comfort zone,' and the numerous replay monitors 'will put an end to the sprints for the best view of that shot off the crossbar.' The downstairs writing and interview rooms are situated at dressing-room level, thus ending 'another trek for reporters' and saving 'precious minutes against a fast-closing deadline.' There are even elevators to carry reporters to the hockey press box: 'The dark days of trudging up endless flights of stairs, hauling laptops and notebooks and telephones, are over for the working press.'

Big City's three major-league teams likewise play in stadia designed to accommodate sports newswork. They are fully equipped with video equipment for instant replays, television monitors so reporters can follow the action, and ubiquitous phone jacks and electrical outlets for ever-present laptop computers and modems – 'the tools of the trade,' one reporter commented. Reporters find these facilities and services at event venues a great advantage largely because they are able to get in touch with their editors immediately. Perhaps a reporter is going to be late filing a story because a game has gone into overtime or had some unexpected delay, or he needs someone back in the newsroom to dig up background information, as well as to confirm rumours heard at the venue while covering the game. The provision of phones and additional phone jacks in the press box also enables reporters to contact sources to obtain quotes and statistics and other background material for stories they may be working on while a game is under way. These seemingly simple services are in fact extremely useful because they save reporters precious time, allowing them to complete much of their news-gathering and story writing in the press box; they can both cover a game as it unfolds and work on other stories as required.

Another interesting service the CFL and NHL teams provide reporters with is 'runners.' Similar to parliamentary pages or newspaper copy chasers, runners distribute information to the press box; mostly this consists of game statistics and other factual details, but also includes scores from the other games around the league that night that can be useful material to include in a game story. Reporters covering the CFL home football games regularly receive updated game statistics, distributed in the press box at the end of each quarter: 'This lets the print guys write their stories as the game goes on, which is important because by the time the game is over, they don't have a whole lot of time before they have to file their stories.' This sort of service helps reporters cope with the demanding pressures of meeting the *Examiner*'s writing deadline. The continuous supply of information reaching reporters in the press box enables them to write their stories as the game progresses. All they have to do at game end to complete their story, aside from routine editorial revisions, is get the requisite quotes from the athletes and coaches. One sportswriter calls this 'rent-a-quote': 'Basically, when the game is over I know what the story is; I've usually written it by the time I go to the locker room. So, all I need to get is a few quotes from the players and coaches, the usual stuff: "We gave it 100 per cent," or "We never quit out there today," you know, the stuff you always read. It's like renting a quote, because you always get the same thing from them.' This comment underscores the importance of quoting athletes and coaches when writing sports news. Indeed, quotes are the 'meat and potatoes' of a reporter's work, the stuff that injects colour and life, emphasis and credibility into a story. Even if what is said is lame, trite, unimaginative, a cliché, reporters *must* get quotes from athletes and coaches. (I will return to this last point in the next chapter when I discuss the personal relations that characterize the relations between reporters and their routine sources.)

Another routine service major-league sports teams provide the media is *pre-game catered meals*. For example, as part of an ongoing effort to build positive relations with major sports media, the National Basketball Association (NBA) makes sure that all its franchises put on elaborate spreads for media types and other VIPs. The Toronto Raptors recently offered an all-you-can-eat buffet of Caesar salad, cannelloni, fried fish, scalloped potatoes, rolls, and chocolate cake. While some NBA franchises charge a small fee (the Vancouver Grizzlies charge reporters $5.00 for their meal), at most games, including the Raptors', the food is free.[12]

In Big City, this pre-game meal service is provided free of charge by the CFL organization, while the NHL team charges a nominal five dollars. During the game, press-box dwellers are treated to a continuous supply of free coffee, soft drinks, bottled water, and popcorn. A veteran media relations staffer explains the rationale behind the practice: 'We try to make things as hospitable as possible for the media guys. A lot of these guys will be working their shift right up to 4 or 5 o'clock and then come flying down to the stadium and don't get a chance to get something to eat. It just makes it easier for them because they don't have to stop and grab something to eat; they can come right to the stadium and get to work. It just helps them do their job, in a small way.' Without having to stop for a meal, reporters can drive directly to the arena or stadium, arriving well before the scheduled start of the event. This is important because the extra time enables reporters to do a lot of the legwork necessary to cover a major commercial sports event, such as doing pre-game interviews, going over the teams' statistics and season highlights packages prepared by media relations staff, and identifying player match-ups to follow during the game.

Moreover, it is important for reporters to have plenty of time to roam about and talk to different people before an event, because 'you get some really good stuff this way':

There's a lot of scuttlebutt in the hallways before a game ... There's player agents, league officials and general managers all over the place and you'd be amazed at the sort of things you overhear them talking about. Really, it's astounding the number of great stories that have been uncovered simply because a reporter overhears a conversation in a hallway before a game ... You also get some good [information] at the meal, because all these same executive types [player agents and team and league officials] are usually there too, talking business or whatever. It's a good opportunity to corner them for an interview, or at least for some comments on that night's game.

Thus, not only are sports reporters assured of a full stomach when covering one of these major-league sports events, but catered meals afford them an opportunity to go about their newsgathering virtually from the moment they arrive at the venue, collecting information and rumours while they eat with colleagues and team officials – yet another instance of commercial sports organizations working to facilitate sports newswork. Taken together, these services – press releases, press conferences, press boxes at event venues, and the like – combine to make doing sports newswork more manageable. The director of communications for the CFL team accurately sums it up: 'Really, the facilities are there for reporters to do their jobs. Everything they need we make sure it's there for them.' The volumes of information that are literally at reporters' fingertips as a result of all this support helps them to meet the *Examiner*'s demand that they generate copy from their beats every day under fixed deadlines.

Thus, in order to do their work, sports reporters must have ready and frequent access to reliable news sources from which a steady stream of sports news flows – news appealing predominantly to male fans. Major-league sports organizations best meet this need because of the perceived greater public interest in them, and the great extent to which they themselves facilitate newswork.

2. Beat Contacts

The second routine source type on which reporters depend for news material is personal contacts ('inside sources') on their beats. 'The best reporters have the best sources,' remarked one sportswriter. Another commented: 'These guys [beat reporters] have a lot of sources ... That's why they're so good, they get a lot of good information from their sources.' Athletes and coaches, team trainers and equipment managers, front-office staff, player agents, league and individual-team executives – all are vital contacts for *Examiner* sports reporters.

These sources provide what amounts to insider information on the world of big-time sports. Arguably this is the sort of sports news most appealing to readers – it's titillating and sensational. In-fighting among management and players, star athletes demanding exorbitant pay increases or a trade, secret negotiations among owners to impose salary caps, owners threatening to move their franchise to more lucrative markets in the face of poor attendance. This news is desirable because it's exciting to the fan – it goes beyond the usual game story or feature article. Indeed, a metropolitan daily with a reputation for providing this sort of coverage is likely to have a devoted following of predominantly male readers, clearly making it a prime candidate for businesses looking for a publication in which to invest their advertising dollars.

The Daily 'Beat Round'

To get a better sense of why it is so important for reporters to have routine sources *other than media relations people*, I followed *Examiner* sports reporter Buck Colvin, who works the NHL beat, through a typical workday. As Mark Fishman has demonstrated, studying a beat reporter's routine round of activities – what he calls a 'beat round' – reveals a great deal about the routine and 'processual' nature of news construction.[13] Colvin follows this routine of activities on a daily basis throughout the NHL season, making highly regular, carefully scheduled rounds of the same people at the same locations.

Colvin begins a typical day around 9:00 a.m. He first calls his sources to 'find out if anything's going on,' hoping to get some leads from them. As he puts it, 'I'm always looking to see if they've heard any rumours, because that's how you get your best stories – someone on your beat hears something, they tell you and then you follow it up, see if there's anything to it.' On this point, Alan Richman notes that the major 'currency' in sports journalism these days is innuendo and rumour: 'Traditionally, a reporter would track down a rumor until it was proved; these days, the publication of the rumor is considered good enough.'[14]

Once he has completed this initial round of telephone calls, Colvin calls the NHL team's media relations director, Gaston Rouge, to see if he has any information. Again, he is looking to find out if anything important has happened with the team since his contact the day before. 'They may have been talking trade with another team the night before, or maybe someone isn't going on the road trip ... anything that'll make a good story, you know.'

Colvin is looking for information to generate two types of news item: stories and briefs. *Sports stories* tend to be longer items, such as feature-length pieces on star athletes, and are usually located in the first couple of pages of the sports section. *Sports briefs*, by contrast, are very short items, 'you know, small items, tidbits like Joe Blow hurt his toe in practice last night and is a doubtful starter for tonight's game.'

After completing this initial coverage work, that is, getting in touch with his sources to familiarize himself with the beat – 'I get an idea of what kind of a news day it's going to be' – Colvin heads off to the team's practice facility at around 11:00 a.m. On-ice practice usually ends at 12:30 p.m., at which time the players head to the gym to continue their workout, and 'that's when I start to really dig for something.' Colvin meets with the team's coaching staff while the players are in the gym, following up on any rumours he's heard or hunches he may have. "I'll be talking to [the head coach] and tell him, 'Look, I heard [names player] was on the trading block. What's going on with that?" Or maybe [names player] didn't get much playing time in last night's game, so I'll ask the coach or one of his assistants if the guy's been benched or what ... I'm basically trying to get some stories from them, you know.' After meeting with the coaching staff, Colvin waits in the locker room for the players to return, usually at around 1:00 p.m. For the next hour or so, he 'hangs out' with the players, talking to different guys, always looking for a story.

'If I'm working on a feature that day, I do my interview for that feature. So if I'm doing a feature on, say, Anton Smith, from one till two o'clock I'll talk to him. But on most days I'll try to talk to at least four or five players.' When pressed to elaborate on just what sort of information he's looking for from the players, Colvin emphasized the importance of rumours, of whispered tidbits of information that can lead him to a substantial news item: 'I'm always asking them about rumours. You always have to go to the players, because the players always know what's going on. They always act like they don't know what's going on, but they always know what's happening.'

Having completed his daily round of activities with the team, Colvin goes to lunch and then arrives at the *Examiner*'s news-room at around 3:00 p.m., at which time he begins making more phone calls to his sources. Throughout the day, Colvin is constantly in contact with people who may be able to supply him with information about his beat. This is especially the case with out-of-town contacts, who typically are other sportswriters. He explains that obviously the *Examiner* can't afford to fly him all over the continent, to every NHL city, to write stories about the team:

So I always stay in contact with sportswriters in other cities because they've always got something I can use. If the Pittsburgh Penguins are coming into town for a game tomorrow, I may phone Pittsburgh just to see if a guy is injured and listed as day-to-day. I'll ask a Penguins' beat

writer down there what the guy's injury status is – that's good information because I can work it into a story. Or I'll ask what's going on with
Mario Lemieux and how he's been doing ... And I always, always, ask
whether they've [other sportswriters] heard any good rumours. *We love
rumours, so the big thing here is to get the rumours; they make for good
stories.*

Accordingly, Colvin spends a great deal of his work day on the
telephone; in a sense, it's the 'lifeline' to his beat. He indicated
that in a typical day he'll easily make upwards of twenty to thirty
phone calls. When I asked him why he makes so many calls, and
if it is really necessary to spend so much of his workday on the
phone, he replied: 'I have to do this to know what's happening
on my beat, to stay on top of things. If I don't, then I'll get beat
on a story, and like I told you, that's my greatest fear. For me,
meeting deadlines isn't the biggest pressure of my job. The biggest pressure is beating the competition, making sure that
you're first. I mean, I can meet deadlines – to me, it's bigger to
have the story first and the only way you're going to do that consistently is to have good sources and stay in touch with them.'
    Colvin usually wraps up this news-gathering component of
his day around 5:30 or 6:00 p.m. with yet another telephone call
to the NHL team's media relations people, 'just to see if there's
anything else up.' Then he'll set to work on writing his news
items, or complete those he has been working on over the
course of the day. Otherwise, if he has to cover a game that
night, Colvin will head down to the arena an hour or two before
game time and spend the rest of the evening there, covering the
game and writing his stories for the 11:00 p.m. deadline. (Often
he'll produce one long game story and a couple of shorter stories
if there's space available; these short pieces tend to focus on a
specific issue or person.)
    The most important thing to note about Colvin's beat round is
that it enables him to complete a lot of his basic coverage work,
his news-gathering, in one centralized location. On this particular day, the team's practice facility was the source of much of
Colvin's news material. Having accessible sports news material

centralized in one or two locations makes it much easier for reporters to meet their deadlines. Notice that Colvin had to be present at only one place to accomplish much of his basic coverage of the beat – the rest of his news-gathering was accomplished over the telephone from his home in the morning and from his desk at the *Examiner*'s newsroom in the late afternoon.

This 'idealization' of Colvin's beat round shows how vital it is for reporters to have a network of sources and to stay in touch with them.[15] As Colvin suggests, without good sources sports reporters wouldn't be able to do their work: 'Good sources are invaluable! You can't do this job unless you've got good sources.'

There's one guy on the team that I talk to every day during the season; there's a couple I talk to at least three times a week; there's others I talk to once every couple weeks. I'm looking to see if they've heard any rumours, you know, who they might be signing, whether they've heard if the team is after a player from another team. You see, I get this kind of information from players because players talk to agents and agents talk to scouts ... There's three or four NHL scouts I talk to usually every day. I also talk to some other people in the organization every day to find out what's going on.

Without the wealth of news information provided by their sources, *Examiner* sports reporters would not be able to generate the quantities of news demanded of them.

Moreover, having these sources centralized in some fashion – such as in a practice facility or accessible by telephone, as we saw with Colvin's beat round – goes a long way towards helping reporters cope with the exigencies of their work. Sports newswork is more manageable when information sources are centralized, largely because centralization cuts down on travel time, leaving more time for news-gathering and writing – therefore making it easier to cover a beat and, ultimately, to satisfy the expectations of the newspaper.

The benefit of having a diverse group of sources on any beat is mostly a matter of being able to generate a lot of news on a daily basis, news that does not directly serve the promotional interests of a commercial sports organization. Yet these are often the most newsworthy stories – stories of internecine conflict, benchings, star players on the trading block, free-agent movement, the list goes on. It is rare for an organization to release this kind of information until *it* is ready to, lest it jeopardize its own position in these sorts of matters. Pete Dewey offers an example of how this works, drawing from his experience working the baseball beat. Covering the Triple 'A' team means Dewey spends most his time writing the typical game stories, straightforward reporting of the final score, the winning/losing pitchers, a few game highlights. He also writes the requisite player profile stories, commenting on their individual performances as the season progresses, and speculating on who from the team might get called up to the major-league parent organization for a shot at 'the big show.' All of this is standard fare for any beat writer, and much of the raw material needed to write these stories is available from the team's media relations staff and from the players and coaches themselves.

Inside sources come into play for Dewey when they tip him off to something that isn't routine, isn't an expected occurrence on his daily round of activities on the beat, and certainly isn't going to be promoted by the organization. He explains:

If there's something developing, say, attendance for the team starts going down, I'm going to want to try and find out why. If I call the team's PR guy, he'll tell me, 'Well, it's bad weather' or something like that, you know, something they can't control. But maybe it's something to do internally within the organization [like a weak marketing department or management conflict], and that's why attendance is down. So I'll call someone in the organization I know and ask them to see if I can get to the bottom of it. But if I don't have these sources, I get no story.

In this instance, Dewey turns to his inside sources to provide him with the 'real story.' These are typically the 'anonymous sources' that most journalists rely on when writing potentially controversial or damaging stories. This example shows the importance of having a network of sources other than media relations people; reporters certainly cannot rely on the organization to 'air its dirty laundry.'

Colvin underscores this last point when he talks about how valuable his personal contacts are to his work as a beat reporter. 'This is how you get your scoops,' he explains.

Last year I had a good story that [names player] wanted 1.2 million dollars on his next contract. Well, that was a big story and it just so happens I got it from somebody who saw the contract, looked at it, and called me and said, 'Buck, you won't believe what [names player] asked for!' You see, without a source in the organization I never would have got that story. The team's [media relations director] sure as hell wouldn't have given it to me – they wait until they're ready to break that kind of stuff, you know, when it suits them.

Maintaining a broad and diverse network of sources on a sports beat pays off in terms of generating news material of the sort not likely to be revealed by a major-league sports organization of their own accord. Consequently, reporters must be careful they don't slash their own wrists by offending and alienating any of their routine official sources.

As noted sportswriter Rick Telander has observed: 'Beat reporters are useless if nobody talks to them.'[16] Thus, there is a great deal of pressure on sports reporters not only to cultivate close relationships with their sources, but to write news items that will not alienate these invaluable sources.

5

Reporter and Source Relations

When a baseball writer starts chewing tobacco, it's time to get worried.

Stephen Brunt, *Globe and Mail* sportswriter

The major-league sport industry's need for so much media coverage is best understood in relation to the continued growth of 'promotional culture' in Western society.[1] The term promotional culture refers to the pervasive and growing presence of promotional discourse and marketing activity in contemporary society – all of it seeking to create receptive audiences for consumer products, including spectacular entertainments like major-league sport. Moreover, there has been a 'subtle shift' in the content and structure of promotional discourse – 'away from making direct claims about the items being promoted and even away from (rational) argumentation, and towards a reliance on visual images, on stylistic connotations, and particularly on symbolic associations.'[2]

In this regard superstar sports personalities offer the greatest possible name recognition and strongest symbolic connotations and associations by virtue of their ubiquitous media presence. Things have reached such a point that even the distinctly promotional appearances of athletes (and increasingly other sports figures like coaches, team owners, league officials, even teams themselves) have come to be understood as entertainment on their own terms – the line between entertainment and promotion is now blurred beyond recognition. As Gruneau and Whitson point out, when Michael Jordan appears in a Nike promotion he is also promoting basketball, the NBA – and, not least, himself, by adding to his own visibility and marketability as a cultural icon.[3] In cultivating a 'larger than life' public persona, the superstar athlete in particular becomes a promotional signifier of unprecedented influence and value, commanding mind-boggling playing, endorsement, and other promotional salaries.

Yet all this promotion hinges on positive media coverage. It is well and good for sports figures to cultivate rebel and 'bad boy' images – indeed, this is a particularly effective marketing gambit. But only within limits. Aside from very exceptional cases like Charles Barkley and Dennis Rodman, those who step over the line risk losing it all in a public relations disaster. Of course, redemption is always possible for fallen heroes; some are even lucky enough to have several chances, like Dexter Manley, who found short-lived notoriety in the CFL after several drug suspensions snuffed out his celebrated NFL career. But redemption too is dependent on major media campaigns designed to remake or reinvent the fallen hero – a full circle from hero to pariah and back again.

With so much at stake, then, routine sources welcome the arrangement whereby sportswriters rely on them for information – since it is but a short step from reliance to dependence. Sources view this dependence as an opportunity to effect some control over what becomes sports news and how it is reported – essentially, control over their public image. It is an opportunity to ensure they get the kind of positive coverage they want and need.

Advancing the Promotional Agenda

Press releases and news conferences are important tools for advancing an organization's promotional agenda. 'It's up to you as an organization to present the information you want reported in the media,' commented the NHL team's director of media relations. News conferences are a good example. They are important tools used by sources to set the news agenda, or at least have a guiding hand in setting it. The conference format 'allows you to get your message out ... It's something you control,' observes one media relations staffer. Another explained that with the news conference, 'essentially, you're giving all the journalists [attending the conference] the same basic facts, you know, the same story, but it's up to them to put their own angle on it. So you give your facts to them, the stuff you want reported. Then the conference breaks up and there's a scrum with reporters running all over the place interviewing whoever they want. But they all end up with the same basic story, more or less.'

Press releases likewise offer a means by which organizations, through their media relations offices, can effect control over the sports news agenda. 'I can sit down and write a press release and it's the information I want out there ... It's how I get out the message I want through the media,' explained one media relations staffer when asked about the promotional utility of press releases: 'The quotes that are in it are the quotes that I get from management or players or [whomever], and those are often the quotes that are picked up when reporters write stories. So it's really what comes out of this office that a lot of the time gets printed, maybe not my words, but the essence of the information I give them often becomes the basis of a story.'

With all this in mind, consider the spectre of negative publicity: organizations rush to issue news releases or hold news conferences at the first scent of bad publicity in order to preserve their public image. Douglas Frederick, a media relations staffer with Big City's CFL team, suggests that such 'damage control,' is vital to determine as much as possible the 'spin' put on a particular news event by the media. Doing so offers an organization a better chance of controlling the facts of the deviance and how they will be reported in the media – negative points can be downplayed and positive ones highlighted. Frederick elaborates this principle by way of example: 'If one of your players gets busted for drugs or something like that, then you'll call a press conference to respond to that story. You don't want to be perceived negatively in society, it's just not beneficial to your club. So you have to present to the media some sort of alternative to fix things. Of course you don't lie, you try to put a positive spin on it.' As he sees it, 'Negatives are there to be turned into positives, as far as the media goes, and positives are there to be hyped.'

Gaston Rouge makes a similar observation when asked how his media relations staff deals with events that could turn out to be bad publicity for the team.

Well there's two sides to every story. Everything doesn't come down to putting a positive spin on it, but telling the truth. If you don't tell the truth they'll find out, you know, these reporters are professionals and they'll find out if you're lying, and you do not want to get caught lying. So when something bad happens the first thing you do is find out what really happened, you get the facts straight. If it's really bad, you can't really smooth it over. [In such a case] all I can do is ensure we have a position, as an organization, on the issue. I call it crisis management.

As we've already seen, press releases bring to reporters' attention a potential news event that would probably have gone unnoticed – a situation that is anathema to a sports organization trying to get lots of 'good ink.' This is especially the case with non-commercial sports organizations. Press releases are arguably their most important promotional tool, a way of bringing their activities to the attention of sportswriters and editors routinely preoccupied with major-league sports beats.

During my fieldwork at the *Examiner*, the sports desk was regularly swamped with press releases, most issued by non-commercial sports organizations of different sorts. I asked the editor about this and, with a chuckle, he said, 'Oh it never stops, that thing is always going. It's mostly junk but sometimes you get something worth sending someone to cover, or maybe make a couple of phone calls to get the results. We get a lot of our local news that way.' Desker and part-time columnist Sam Snead illustrates how press releases are useful tools for obtaining coverage, especially for local sports organizations that are not regular news subjects: 'Press releases help with some things we don't cover that often ... say the Canadian Broomball Association gives us a release saying that some guy has been named to the North American all-star team and he's from the local area. Well, no one's going to be covering that as part of any beat, so it's good to know that kind of thing, it's good to get a release on it. It's the kind of story that might provide an interesting little sidebar or a small feature or something like that.'

Thanks to the ubiquitous nature of fax technology nowadays (found in printing and photocopy shops, schools, and corner stores, as well as businesses and homes), even the most resource-poor sports organizations have the means to fax press releases to news organizations. 'Oh, we get faxes from every-where you can imagine,' explained the *Examiner*'s sports editor. 'Big league teams, of course, but we also get tons of them from local sports teams ... People pretty much know it's the best way to let us know if something's going on so they can get some coverage. With a lot of the amateur stuff we'd have no idea what was happening if we didn't get a fax or phone call.'

By influencing the sports news agenda through releases and conferences, sources are able to control to a certain extent what is reported and how – they effect control to a great extent over what becomes sports news. Having this sort of control is especially useful to source organizations when they are faced with the possibility of negative publicity. This is why, as we saw in the previous chapter, commercial sports organizations go to great lengths and expense to facilitate sports newswork by issuing lots of press releases and holding news conferences – it is to advance their promotional interests, to secure as much positive coverage of their activities as possible on a regular basis.

The blatantly promotional character of releases and conferences is not lost on the *Examiner*'s sportswriters; for the most part they seem to be fully aware of the major efforts being made to manipulate news content by manipulating *them*. As Leo Rosten observed some sixty years ago in his study of Washington, DC, newspaper correspondents, there are no press releases on the 'failures, scandals, dissentions, and inconsistencies' of an organization.[4] This is most certainly the case today with major-league sports. Indeed, *Examiner* sports newsworkers to a person were generally distrustful of media relations people and their 'obvious agenda.' As one beat reporter observed, 'Most of the newsworthy stuff is never press released because it's usually negative stuff.' As he sees, it only makes sense to treat press releases and other information provided by major-league sports teams with a degree of scepticism, as their promotional interests are contingent upon supplying sports reporters with *positive* news material: 'You know, the [names NHL team] aren't going to send out a press release saying so-and-so had a sordid past in the Soviet Union or something like that. Likewise, the [names Triple 'A' baseball team] aren't going to send out a release saying they lost $500,000 last year. The only press releases you get are about the stuff *they* want you to know.' Another beat reporter makes a similar observation, arguing that sports teams keep potentially negative news under wraps, well away from reporters. He explains that it is simply part of the job to recognize that media relations staffers 'are only going to tell you what they want to come out ... What the PR guy's gonna tell you is that [names player] was named Rookie-of-the-Month. Okay, that's great, but the PR guy's not going to tell you that this guy sent the club a letter saying he wants to renegotiate his contract. They're not gonna tell you that, and obviously it's a bigger story, *it's the real story* ... You don't get this kind of story from a PR guy!'

To counter the distinctly promotional bias of press releases and news conferences, sportswriters work hard to cultivate and maintain an extensive network of personal contacts on their beats. One veteran reporter underscores this point: 'When I say sources, I don't really mean PR guys; sure, they're a good source, they know what's going on. But for the most part they're just promoting their team.' The *real* sources he is alluding to range from the obvious – athletes, coaches, management officials – to the not so obvious – front-office staff, equipment managers and trainers, and player agents. Taken together they coalesce to become vital components of the sports journalism machine, providing huge amounts of information that would not be available to reporters were they to rely solely on media relations people.

Another sportswriter elaborated on the need for a diverse network of beat contacts. When asked how important it is to have sources other than media relations people on a beat, his response was unequivocal: 'They're the ones that provide you the information, I mean, you can't rely on information from the PR people ... Real sources are different from PR people, they're not team flunkies. They're totally different because PR people are only going to tell you what they want to get out. Sources, they're people that, whoever it may be, are people who may be associated with the team, or might know a player. They give you rumours, you know, and we check them out ... It would be tough to do the job without them. I mean, they're the ones that give you the information.'

Venerable Montreal Canadiens beat reporter Rejean Tremblay has loudly complained in a column that the Canadiens' management granted the media *too much* access to players in an attempt to effect spin control. He complained: 'They will tell you everything but the truth. They will tell you everything is going right when it isn't. They have a message and they get it out. Is it the truth? No. But it becomes the truth when we write it. It becomes the truth when we put our bylines on it.'[5]

In brief, sportswriters can't count on media relations staffers to provide them with much in the way of news material that may be controversial to the extent it may put the organization or any of its people in a bad light – yet these are often the most newsworthy stories. And since reporters cannot very well expect a source to cut its own throat by exposing its shortcomings, 'you must have sources who are willing to do so.'

The necessity for having a coterie of reliable news sources other than media relations people must not be underestimated; reporters most certainly cannot rely on an organization to 'air its dirty laundry.' Reporters could not possibly generate this kind of material were it not for their personal contacts on the beat: 'If I don't have these sources, I get no story,' is how one veteran sportswriter summed it up. Recall the point made by Rick Telander at the end of the previous chapter: 'Beat reporters are useless if nobody talks to them.'[6]

The upshot of all this is that *Examiner* sportswriters are under a great deal of pressure to cultivate close relationships with their beat contacts. In return for cultivating a close relationship with a coach, for instance, a favoured reporter may be given a news tip not necessarily made available to others, thus enabling the beneficiary of such largesse to steal a march on his colleagues: 'If you do the coach a favour he will give you a news story when you require one, tip you off to something that is happening.'[7] In return for such 'news favours,' sportswriters are likely to reciprocate with favourable copy – perhaps playing up a team's performance when it is in a slump, writing a feature story on an athlete, or promoting an upcoming sports event – in their articles and columns.

However, reporters must not only cultivate close relationships with their sources on the sports beat, but they must also be careful not to alienate themselves from these sources by writing stories to which their sources might take offence. Indeed, sportswriters must walk a fine line when writing stories that could potentially offend their sources; a balance must be struck between maintaining positive relations with sources and upholding the journalistic principle of objectivity.

The Question of Objectivity

A number of writers have called into question sportswriters' objectivity in light of the ostensibly 'cozy' nature of their relations with routine sources. It seems only natural to expect beat reporters to identify, to a certain extent, with their routine sources given the vast amounts of time they spend with them. Arguably this is especially the case with sports reporters. As Cumming and McKercher observe, a police reporter is likely to check in with key sources almost every day, often by phone. But when the shift is over, the reporter and officer go their separate ways. By contrast, a sportswriter covering a team 'may spend weeks on the road with the coaches and athletes, seeing them at all hours and in all circumstances, from the first practice of the morning to the closing of the last bar at night.'[8] They conclude

that, over time, the writer will more than likely develop an affection for the players as individuals and the team as a whole, and
'perhaps even to identify with them.' It is precisely these sentiments that major-league sports organizations and prominent
sports figures seek to cultivate and subsequently exploit.

Veteran sportswriter Dick Beddoes illustrates the conse-
quences of this state of affairs for news content in the sports
pages. Writing in the early 1970s, he laments the relatively poor
quality of sports journalism: 'I believe there still is a tendency
among sports reporters to slant news in favour of the home team,
to defer to local sports management for the sake of maintaining
cordial working relationships, and to accept publicity handouts
in place of digging for their own stories.' Most of the *slanting* Beddoes refers to 'comes from too-close association with the coach,
who throws a bone to the reporters every few days so they will
have something fresh to write about,' then 'expects the reporters
to give him a break when the going gets rough.'[9]

With this point in mind, I asked *Examiner* sportswriter Chet
Burkley if he ever feels that his objectivity is compromised by the
necessity of maintaining such close relations with his sources,
the very subjects he is expected to report on critically. Without a
doubt, he noted, 'it gets tough when you have to write something about a guy that you know he isn't going to like ... Usually
they know I'm just doing my job, but some guys really take it
personal if I trash them in the paper, you know, they won't talk
to me anymore. This has actually happened to me with a university football coach ... I really don't want to piss off my sources
because then they won't talk to me.' At the end of the day, walk-
ing this tightrope is 'just part of my job ... In the end you're
gonna piss people off no matter what.'

In short, *Examiner* sportswriters must be careful not to offend
their routine sources. For those who are too critical too often,
retaliation can be swift and vicious.

Source Sanctions

Now I want to examine more closely the sanctions that routine
sources impose on sportswriters who fail to serve their promo-

tional objectives on a regular basis. There are two general types to consider: (1) physical sanctions and, most effective, (2) the cutting-off of access.

Physical Sanctions

An athlete or coach who does not approve of a story, for example, may well accost the sportswriter in the clubhouse the next day. Following a Toronto Maple Leafs hockey game, Mike Nykoluk, a Leafs assistant coach, having taken exception to some editorial barbs thrust at his 'indifferent coaching' by the *Globe and Mail*'s Al Strachan, grabbed Strachan and shoved him from the Leafs dressing room. 'You start running me down, you son of a bitch ... and I don't want you in here. Now get the fuck out 'cause you're no goddamn sports writer!'[10]

Telander suggests that athletes can also 'intimidate without touching,' as when a major-league baseball player 'ominously' pointed his bat at a reporter and warned, 'You stay away from me!'[11] And Alan Richman writes of an incident where the response to a sportswriter's innocent question – 'Kirk, can I talk to you for a minute?' – was a flood of verbal abuse from the athlete and the threat of physical harm.[12]

I was told of only one incident involving a rather extreme physical sanction levied by athletes against an *Examiner* sportswriter. Chet Burkley related an incident involving Big City's CFL team, where the *Examiner*'s beat reporter, Bobby Barnes, had written a feature on the team towards the latter part of the season. The article was basically a 'report card' type of item, where Barnes graded the team's performance to date on a position-by-position basis. Writing such an item is 'always tough because nobody's going to be happy, they'll all think they should have done better than how you grade them.' The day after the article appeared in the *Examiner*, Barnes was at the team's clubhouse going through his regular beat round,

when the players basically surrounded him in the dressing room and tried to intimidate him, you know, somebody threw a great big container of water on him ... He was pretty intimidated, because he was there all alone, basically the team and him. Technically he could have charged them with assault, but you'd never do that. The next day he wrote a column, real tongue-in-cheek, saying something like, 'Sorry, I didn't realize that the worst team in the CFL deserved all A's on their report card.' Anyway, you're gonna piss people off, sure, but that's going way too far.

Although this demonstrates the extreme that sources go to in exacting retribution against a reporter who has offended them, bear in mind that this was an exceptional case. Most of the newsworkers and media relations staffers I interviewed were hard-pressed to recall any incidents as extreme. What I found to be a more typical form of sanction than a punch in the nose was a refusal by offended sources to facilitate newswork – a refusal to provide access to a steady flow of raw news material. This is especially the case with athletes.

Cutting Access to Routine Sources

Commercial sports organizations, as we've already seen, have an interest in being portrayed in a positive light – a truism of our promotional culture. One thing they strive to do is cultivate and maintain a 'professional' image, that of a top-notch professional sports organization able to deliver 'high-quality entertainment.' Thus, any sort of coverage that tarnishes this image is certainly not welcomed by the organization; they don't want the kind of bad publicity a negative news item constitutes and move swiftly to make reporters aware of this fact. For example, an Associated Press story (March 1995) reported that a Canton, Ohio, newspaper returned its press credentials for the 1995 Canton-Akron Indians baseball season after being told the passes would be revoked if the paper ran unflattering stories about the Double 'A' Eastern League team. In a letter to the paper's sports editor, the Indians' general manager wrote: 'At the point a negative article about the franchise appears anywhere in your paper, your credentials will be revoked and you will be asked to purchase a ticket and cover the games from outside the press box.'

The paper said 'no thanks' to the press credentials and instead opted to pay admission to the stadium and have its sportswriters cover the game from the stands rather than be subject to such intimidation.

More recently, the head coach of the CFL's Calgary Stampeders instructed everyone affiliated with his club to refrain from speaking to *Globe and Mail* sportswriter Marty York, after York wrote a series of unflattering stories about former Stampeder quarterback Doug Flutie.[13] The team's marketing and communications director said that 'he and his co-workers are under strict orders from [head coach Wally] Buono to no longer answer questions' from York because of what the general manager / head coach considered to be 'less-than-favourable stories' York had written in the previous off-season about the former Stamps quarterback. Interesting to note, aside from the coach's deliberate attempt to sanction a reporter who was writing stories he didn't like, was the team owner's reaction to the situation. Sid Gutsche said he felt Buono was clearly out of line in instructing personnel not to talk to York – such action flies directly in the face of the team's promotional interests, its need for lots of positive press coverage. 'If I stopped talking to everyone who criticized me,' Gutsche said, 'I wouldn't have anyone to talk to ... In our position, we can't afford to be rejecting potential publicity, and I intend to have [Buono] review this policy quickly. We need all the attention we can get.'

As for *Examiner* sportswriters, several have been sanctioned by various major-league sports clubs for failing to write positive stories. One explained how two years previous he had written a story revealing that a Junior 'A' hockey player, upon learning he had been traded to the local Junior 'A' club, had decided instead to play in a professional league on the east coast: 'I wrote about that and I got in trouble from the junior hockey team's PR person. He gave me crap for writing about something negative when I should have been writing about positive stuff, like a big upcoming game or something.'

Pete Dewey recounted a similar experience he'd had while working his baseball beat during the team's first season in Big

City. At one point during the 1993 season he wrote an ostensibly critical article about how crowded the team's bus was on a road trip, how players were complaining about having to sit in the aisles and on equipment bags at the back of the bus. The story implied the ball club was 'a bit of a Mickey Mouse' operation – clearly not the sort of image the organization wanted the press to promote. Dewey picks up the narrative:

Anyway, about a week after that story ran, there was a big meeting after a game in the manager's office, but I wasn't allowed in. I thought maybe there was a big trade in the making or something like that. After the meeting, they said for us [reporters] to come in and sit down. The manager, the general manager, and the [major-league affiliate's] minor-league director were there. They said, 'You can't write stuff like that ... you can't write about the bus' and 'We're thinking about not letting you on the bus anymore [to travel with the team]' ... So this year there's a new manager, and they don't allow us on the bus if there's no flying involved on the trip. So they're going down to Scranton and it's all bus, but we're not allowed on so I have to drive it, I guess.

As a result of writing this negative news item, Dewey was banned from accompanying the team on its road trips, at least to the extent of travelling with the players.[14] So what appeared to be a fairly innocuous story turned out to be a real contentious one from the perspective of the baseball team.

I want to be careful not to overstate the case: although commercial sports organizations are indeed important routine sources for reporters (recall all the trouble and expense they go to facilitate sports newswork), it would take an extreme breach of their relationship for a major-league sports organization to completely cut a reporter off – it is simply not in their promotional interests to do so. As I've already noted several times, major-league sports need the regular publicity media coverage affords them: the sports business depends on the advertising afforded by news coverage, and the promoter doesn't want to put obstacles in the way of those who supply it.[15]

The National Basketball Association has instituted a policy

designed to ensure the media have extensive access to players and coaches. Reporters can interview players for forty-five minutes before and after every game, and the league fines any athletes and teams that do not cooperate. For example, in May 1997, the NBA fined the Chicago Bulls $25,000 for failing to make players available after a practice. This fine was doubled a few weeks later for a second offence. The NBA also fined superstars Michael Jordan and Charles Barkley $10,000 apiece for not showing up to an All-Star Game press conference.[16]

One veteran media relations staffer, when asked if he had ever sanctioned a reporter for writing a news item he felt was too negative or unfair, explained that he never had, nor would he ever, 'freeze out' a reporter for writing negative stories. 'Even if you don't like the guy, you think he's irresponsible or a sensationalist ... your job is to maximize the coverage of your team.' Commercial sports organizations will not sever their relations with a reporter simply because they need the coverage too much to take such drastic action. Reporters can expect, in fact, they can pretty much count on, a major-league sports organization to supply them with news material even after they've been critical of the team or its management in print.

Examiner sportswriters are very much aware of this state of affairs. One explains that it's extremely unlikely that any major-league sports organization would compromise its promotional interests in order to punish a recalcitrant reporter: 'You'd never get a PR guy cutting you off. They'll always send you releases and invite you to conferences because they can't afford not to. If they're pissed off because you wrote something they didn't like, you know, you said they sucked, or whatever, they've still got to do their job because if they don't, you can just write about that, that they're an amateur organization, that they're hiding from the media, whatever. You see, that's bad publicity for them, too. It's a no winner for them that way.' Burkley similarly observes that it is simply not in the organization's best interests to withhold news material for the sake of punishment or making a point. He, like his colleagues, is well aware of the fundamental nature of sports promotion, noting of media relations staffers that 'it's their job to feed us information ... They won't cut you off for writing negative stuff, they can't. I mean, if we didn't write it as we see it, we'd lose our readers because [our readers] know if the team isn't playing well. If all we wrote were positive stories, then we'd lose a lot of credibility with our readers. So, what I mean is they expect that we'll write negative stories, it's just the way it is. So it wouldn't do them any good to ban me from their locker room just because I write a piece criticizing management or whatever.' Sportswriters, especially those responsible for a beat, are far more concerned with losing access to their network of personal contacts. This is the sanction they fear most.

To be cut off from the flow of 'inside information' that routine beat contacts provide would be disastrous. As one veteran sportswriter put it: 'You're [in real trouble] if you're good sources won't talk to you ... You've got to have them! If you want anything good, you've got to have good sources. I see my job as having to know everything that's happening with my team, so I have to have the players, coaching staff and management trust me and tell me stuff on and off the record that they know I'm not going to screw them on. I want them to feel like they can confide in me and they can tell me what's going on.' Another explained, regarding his beat contacts, that 'the worst thing I could do would be to piss off my sources, because if I do, then they aren't going to talk to me and then I'm basically screwed ... I need people who are willing to tell me what's going on; who are willing to tell me ... if there's going to be a trade, if somebody's going to make a move, if somebody's going to be sitting out of the line-up, that kind of stuff.' And a third reporter made similar comments regarding the importance of having a network of personal sources on the beat, and the necessity of not offending them:

Your contacts on the beat are incredibly important – the best reporters are the ones with the best sources. If you have people on the inside who can tell you what's going on, that's good stuff, that's how you get the good stories. For example, players know everything; they know what's going on. People think players are left in the dark, but no, the players know everything. If you have good contacts with the players, you know, a friendly relationship, they're the guys who are gonna say that 'management or league officials are trying to mess us around,' or whatever the story may be.

Thus, while the threat of a beating at the hands of a disgruntled athlete or coach may be real (though unlikely), sports reporters are more likely to receive the 'cold shoulder' in response to an unflattering news story. Based on his experience as a sportswriter, Rick Telander says it goes as follows:

Player reads story and is upset; writer returns to locker room to find player mute. If the writer is lucky enough to coax an explanation from the athlete, he/she will hear that the story was unfair because it did at least one of the following: (a) misquoted the athlete; (b) used his quotes out of context; (c) used off-the-record material; (d) mentioned his private life; (e) misinterpreted his philosophy, salary, attitude, or childhood; (f) portrayed him as a bad person; (g) portrayed him as a bad athlete.[17]

Telander's model is illustrated nicely by the storm of controversy caused in the 1994 CFL regular season over league commissioner Larry Smith's decision to cover the Hamilton Tiger Cats' payroll on a week when the team couldn't afford to do so – only a week after Smith told reporters that the league would in no way use its funds for such a bail-out.[18] The limited partnership operating the cash-strapped team was at the time headed by Toronto financier David MacDonald, who refused to respond to a reporter's questions as to how the players and staff would be paid for the rest of the year: 'I don't comment on private matters ... I'm not going confirm or deny anything to you. I don't ask how big your T4 is, do I?' MacDonald continued to berate the reporter, threatening, 'If you continue to write negative stories about the Ticats and the CFL, you and [Globe and Mail sports reporter] Stephen Brunt and the reporter who writes for Canadian Press will all be out of jobs. There won't be any football to cover [because the league will fold].' Clearly, MacDonald attempted to use his position as an important news source to bully reporters into giving both the team and the league favourable coverage. His comments imply that anything short of this would spell the end of not only the Ticats but the whole Canadian Football League.

Another good illustration of how sources try to control news coverage occurred during the NHL lockout, when *Winnipeg Free Press* sports columnist Scott Taylor aligned himself firmly with management, supporting the owners' contention that a salary cap was needed to keep the small-market clubs in business and expressed this opinion regularly in his column.[19] At one point Taylor walked into the Winnipeg Jets' locker room and received an icy reception from the players. To a man, they refused to talk to him, and noted NHL bad boy Tie Domi 'attached the F-word to a description of Taylor (within earshot) that likened him to a body orifice.' A meeting was subsequently held with club officials and four players, 'during which the sides aired their differences.' According to a source close to the team, the skirmish was caused by the players' perception that Taylor 'was too close to [club owner Barry] Shenkarow.'

Further support for Telander's model of source sanctions is found in Smith and Valeriote's study of ethics in sports journalism.[20] They report a situation where a reporter wrote an article describing how a hockey player had been 'drunk and acted boorishly on the team's flight home.' Although the story was true, 'the athletes subsequently refused to talk to the reporter.' As a result, the reporter's 'sources of information had dried up,' the players on the team refusing to speak to him, and the paper changed his assignment. Without reliable access to sources able to supply a steady flow of news material, sports reporters are useless to their paper.

Recalcitrant sports reporters, those who regularly adopt a critical stance in their reporting that does not serve a source's promotional interests, may find themselves barred from a team's clubhouse or faced with uncooperative players and coaches. For example, the late Harold Ballard, owner of the Toronto Maple Leafs, used to cultivate a handful of reporters by rewarding them with exclusive interviews that were often controversial and therefore sure to 'score points' for the reporter who 'dug them up.' He also rewarded sportswriters who were especially deep in his hip pocket with access to the team's clubhouse and players beyond that available to most reporters. Conversely, those who wrote items offensive to Ballard were dismissed with a curt 'Fuck 'em!' and missed out on his largesse.[21]

This *symbiosis*, wherein sports reporters are driven to pander to the interests of their sources by virtue of their reliance on these sources for news material, led one sports columnist to complain:

I just know that it can't go on like this much longer. The media and the [CFL] players' association must bury the hatchet ... There could and should be a natural weeding out process, rather than that blanket attitude by some players toward the media.

If a writer is constantly guilty of misquoting players or a broadcaster, in editing a tape, uses that clip which invariably is a stumbling answer to a tough question, then he or she should be ostracized. But if a writer or broadcaster isn't involved in those games, he or she should be entitled to the time of day, not be ducked by a player only as a matter of principle.[22]

The experience of being sanctioned for writing what their sources consider to be negative news items was relatively common among the *Examiner*'s sportswriters. Consider the following interview excerpts:

They may not talk to you, but that usually only goes on for a few days, in my experience.

You're always gonna piss off your sources at one time or another. Usually they just won't talk to you for a while, they'll ignore you, you know, not return your calls, tell you nothing's going on [with the beat] when really there is, that sort of bullshit.

Well most of them will say, 'That's the last time I'm telling you anything,' and then after a while cooler heads prevail. For example, one of the defenceman [for the NHL team] I talk to a lot, he says to me one time: 'Why'd you bag me in the paper!' And I says back to him, 'Because that's my job. You know you played bad, I know you played bad, and you can't hide from the 10,000 people who saw you play bad, too.' They'd laugh my ass out of town if I didn't write that the guy played like hell.

If it's a bad enough story, they'll probably tell you to go screw yourself next time they see you. They may also never speak to you again, or at least threaten not to; I've had that happen to me. Or at least, you'll never get a tip-off from them about anything, that's for sure.

The common thread running through these quotations is that sources react to negative coverage – thus, negative publicity – by threatening to cut off the offending reporter's access to the raw news material they need to do their work. The reasoning here is premised on the simple notion that reporters will be more inclined to write positive news items if they feel their access to a reliable source of information is threatened by doing otherwise. One veteran sportswriter explained that it is indeed 'very diffi-cult' to write a negative story when it's likely to offend a routine news source: 'It's tough when you've got to write something about one of your sources and you know it's going to really piss them off. The good ones understand I'm just doing my job and I'm going to treat them fairly. But some of them, especially play-ers, go nuts, you know, "What the hell did you write that for! You're not getting anything from me again!"'

If a source manages to sway a reporter away from writing a potentially damaging story by threatening to cut off access to the source in the future, then the source has managed to exert some control over what becomes sports news. It is possible that some news items will be suppressed based on a source's potentially volatile reaction to them. This is done to protect their public personae as sports celebrities. Because 'the best reporters are the ones with the best sources,' they must think long and hard about writing a story that may cost them one of the important sources in their stable.

When asked to talk about the biggest news story he'd broken in his career, Buck Colvin offers a nice illustration of just how vital the inside information beat contacts provide sportswriters is:

You depend on your sources so much, because PR guys are only gonna tell you what they want to come out. For example, the biggest story I ever got was that the Board of Directors for the [names CFL team] had resigned, and nobody knew. There were rumours flying all around, and nobody was looking into it. So we were at the ball game one night and I said to [Examiner colleague] Bobby Barnes, 'Something's going on, keep your eye on the game, I gotta go check it out.'

So I go down to the president's box and ask him what's going on. I say, 'The CFL's got a meeting in Toronto on Friday and the rumour is you guys [the Board of Directors] have resigned.' And he says he's got no comment, the CFL commissioner will make a statement then. I say, 'Fine, but off-the-record what's going on?' He tells me he can't say anything. So I had another source on the Board of Directors and I went to him and he said, 'Look, Buck, we've all resigned, we've stepped down, and the CFL is going to say tomorrow that it is taking over the team.' And I'm thinking, Holy shit, this is big, so I write it up. The next day it was the biggest story in the city, in the country, and we had it.

This quote illustrates just how important a reporter's network of personal beat contacts is; obviously league officials and the team's management were not willing to break such a major news item until they were ready to do so. It took confirmation of a rumour from an inside source to break the story.

Significantly, because Colvin had an inside source with the organization, he was able to scoop all of Big City's sports journalists on this major story – a big deal, as he explained in a subsequent interview. 'The biggest thing for a reporter is to win: it's our game, you know. The players have their game on the ice and we have our game off the ice. If I can scoop [everyone else] that makes me real happy. There's nothing better than the kill.' Without a network of contacts on the beat, however, Colvin would never have broken this, 'the biggest story' of his career – he would never have made 'the kill.'

Sports reporters clearly depend on their contacts to provide them with a lot of potential news items on any given day. Recall the earlier discussion of Colvin's beat round with his NHL team. He culls news material every day by talking to the players and coaches, collecting the rumours and tips that constitute raw news materials. Without these sources – if Colvin were to be frozen out, his contacts refusing to talk to him – he'd be left out in the cold and thus unable to do his job. If a contact is offended because Colvin has written a negative item about him, or breaks a story and then implicates the contact as a key source, thereby breaking a confidence between them, then the contact is likely to respond by severing relations with Colvin.

I asked Bernie Krusher, who is head coach of a university football team, to characterize his relations with the local sports journalists, how he experiences his role as a fairly routine news source.[23] He explains that 'when it comes right down to it, if you object to a reporter's line of questioning, or how they've conducted an interview,' a source is perfectly justified in refusing to cooperate with the offender in the future.

Now, I'm not in a position to say, 'You can't speak to our players,' because I think the reporter is entitled to contact them and speak to them. But what it comes down to for me is, it's a personal thing, and it's only happened to me once before. I came to a point where I indicated [to a hectoring reporter] I was no longer interested in speaking to him about a particular issue. But that came about only after at least two or three opportunities where I indicated my concerns to this individual and it never changed.

So when his line of questioning and approach didn't change after I expressed my concerns, I thought, 'I'm not interested in being a source, in continuing to provide information which then allows this individual to repeatedly report in this fashion.' So I just said to him, 'I'm not interested in speaking to you any further.' And I have not had a phone call from him since, although the individual is still reporting.

In effect, the offended contact refuses to facilitate newswork. As Krusher explains,

If you like somebody, you're apt to go out of your way to make sure you're assisting them in any way; whether it's giving them statistics, giving them extra details, calling them up when you feel there's a story that maybe they're not aware of that you think they may be interested in. And I've done that ... I do it because we'll benefit in terms of getting some good coverage, and reporters benefit because I've provided them with a good story. For example, I'll call up a reporter and say, 'Did you know that so-and-so has won this award? It's not public knowledge yet, but it's okay to be released and I'm calling you up to let you know.' And then they would begin a story on this. Whereas if you're a reporter that's come in and you've repeatedly ticked me off, then definitely in your line of questioning I'm going to answer, I'm going to be courteous, I'm going to try and do my job and be fair about it. But you're going to find shorter answers; you're not going get the extra details; you're not going to get the phone call from me saying that something newsworthy has happened with our team and I wanted to let you know about it.

Krusher highlights the point that sources use access to inside information as a sanction. Although he would not totally cut off a recalcitrant reporter – 'I'd never do that because he'll just write something bad about that ... about me cutting him off' – he would not, however, facilitate that person's work to any appreciable degree.

Thus, the impact of severing relations with a reporter is significant, because it means the reporter has lost an important source of information on his or her beat: someone they can turn to when they need something on a slow news day; someone to provide them with tips and rumours, and so on. Sources are more inclined to facilitate the sports newswork of a reporter whom they believe treats them fairly.

Interestingly, to some sources 'fairness' means writing positive sports copy – of the sort that will contribute to their promotional interests – rather than producing a balanced, objective, and journalistically sound news item. Concerning major-league sports organizations, one sportswriter remarked quite cynically, 'Fairness to a PR flak means writing stories that will sell tickets.

They seem to have the opinion that we're in this all together ...
and we should work together to sell the product. But it just
doesn't work that way.' In any event, sources who have been
offended in one way or another by a reporter react by 'going for
the jugular' – they threaten the reporter's news supply and, ultimately, his or her ability to do their job. One of the main problems this poses for sportswriters is that they can't get interview
quotes for their stories, a staple of contemporary sports journalism. Leonard Koppett laments that contemporary sports journalism suffers from its slavish adherence to 'the cult of the
quote,' characterized by editors telling their reporters to, above
all else, 'Get quotes ... Lots of quotes.' The consequence: reporters preoccupied with 'stalking quotes as if with a butterfly net.'[24]

Where this all leads, of course, is full circle back to where we
began: whether sportswriters quote them or not, they are
obliged to talk to beat contacts to find anything out; this is their
job, it's how they make a living. And since there is no way to get
information and quotes except by talking to the people involved,
if they won't talk, 'you're in real trouble.' Sportswriters can ill
afford to have their information sources dry up on them. If beat
sources sever relations with sports reporters, for whatever rea-
sons, it is next to impossible for the victim to do his or her work.
Reporters need the tip-offs and rumours from athletes, coaches,
secretaries, equipment managers, trainers, and front-office staff;
they depend on unfettered access to athletes and coaches for the
all-important interview. Without all this, a reporter is of little use
to their newspaper, and it wouldn't be long before she or he
would be looking for work elsewhere. Recalling the words of
Telander, 'Beat reporters are useless if nobody talks to them.'

The result of this web of relations between sports reporter and
source is this: major-league sports organizations and individual
athletes institutionalize contacts with reporters, creating a
bridge between themselves and the reading public who consume the sports entertainment product. By exploiting their relationships with reporters, sources succeed in garnering the lion's
share of column space in the sports section of metropolitan
daily newspapers to promote their product.

6

In Whose Interests?
Sports News and the Question
of Ideology

The trouble with ideology, Alice, is that it hates the private. You must
make it human.

Michael Ondaatje, *In the Skin of a Lion*

The sociologist Dorothy Smith argues that news is ideological
because it is produced through 'procedures people use as a
means not to know.'[1] This is especially the case with sports news,
as we've seen throughout this book. The routine work practices
and professional ideologies that constitute sports newswork –
while eminently successful in capturing the goings-on of the
major-league commercial sports world with precision and in
admirable detail – are principally a 'means not to know' about
another, more expansive world: the world of non-commercial
spectator sports.

The economic logic of the daily press demands that the range
of coverage in the sports pages be restricted almost exclusively to
major-league spectator sports. Metropolitan daily newspapers
are primarily advertising-supported, depending on advertising
sales and not circulation to generate the bulk of their revenue.
Accordingly, a quality readership demographic that is appealing
to advertisers must be cultivated, one that is clearly defined and
highly concentrated. The prevailing philosophy in the news business is that a quality sports readership is an eighteen- to forty-

nine-year-old, male-dominated demographic. And the approach taken by the *Examiner* to attract this highly sought-after audience is to provide extensive coverage of major commercial sports such as the CFL, NFL, NBA, NHL, and so on – the cash cows that 'deliver the male.' The paper's sports section is thus regularly saturated with coverage of the commercial sports world as a matter of economic necessity.

The burden of generating this sports news every day falls on the shoulders of the paper's sports reporters – and this work is carried out in an environment rife with pressures and constraints. The *Examiner* employs a 'beat system' of reporting that obliges sports reporters to generate fresh copy from these beats daily; this is a normative requirement of the job. In other words, the whole point of the reporter's beat work is to generate commercial sports news to fill the paper's sports section each day. The high premium placed on producing this sort of sports news is evidenced by the fact that responsibility for covering a beat carries with it an obligation to write something every day about that beat – this is not negotiable. Thus, a perceived lack of 'newsworthy' activity on a sports beat is insufficient grounds for a reporter not to produce any news. And to make matters worse, reporters have to write their news items under impending deadlines ostensibly beyond their control. To cope with these exigencies of sports newswork, reporters must have reliable access to steady flows of raw news material; this is the only way they can do their work under such trying conditions.

In this sense, sports newswork is an extremely routine activity – to the extent that reporters depend on routine news sources to provide the bulk of their news material on a daily basis. Almost invariably these routine sources are from the commercial sports world: media relations staffers and management personnel of large sports organizations, and personal contacts on the beat, including coaches and athletes, agents, and so on. Sports reporters depend on these routine sources for the bulk of their sports news material, and they work hard to cultivate and maintain close relations with them.

The upshot of all this is that sports news carries a great deal of ideological freight. And Smith's valuable insight – that newswork is constituted by a series of procedures that are a means not to know certain regions of the social world – forces the fundamental question on which the critique of ideology must hang: In whose interests?

I find it most useful to think of the concept 'ideology' in terms of legitimating the power of a dominant group or social class. In this sense, to study ideology is to 'study the ways in which meaning (or signification) serves to sustain relations of domination.'[2] A successful ideology is one that succeeds in rendering its own vested interests natural and self-evident – to be identified with the 'common sense' of a society so that nobody could imagine how things might ever be different. Ideology, from this perspective, presents itself as an 'Of course!' or 'That goes without saying' or 'That's just the way things are, there's nothing you can do about it' – it freezes itself into a 'second nature,' presenting itself as completely natural, inevitable, and thus *unalterable*.[3]

Sports news is ideological precisely because it constitutes a discourse that serves the promotional interests of the major-league sports industry's primary stakeholders – team owners, media commentators, equipment and apparel manufacturers, civic boosters, and the like. This means that in the sports press there is little room for news that doesn't promote the industry. After all, you don't create a positive atmosphere of consumption with a lot of critical news of the sort that calls into question the fundamental nature and functioning of the sports industry. This notion of 'consumption' is crucial to my argument that the sports section is the nearly exclusive *promotional domain* of the big-time sports business.

As I've tried to show throughout this book, the prevailing philosophy among sports newsworkers is that consumers want to read about their favourite major-league sports teams and celebrities; moreover, the sort of news they perceive that readers want to have is of the 'gossipy' insider sort, along with the traditional game stories laden with banal clichés uttered by key players and coaches. By extension, the sports section is regarded as a place to escape from the drudgeries of everyday life – a sphere that, the argument runs, ought to be free from the highly critical and often negative reporting characteristic of political and crime news coverage; it should be entertaining above all else.

The sports section is a finely tuned, high-performance promotional vehicle for the North American (and increasingly global) sports entertainment industry. As long as the sports press continues to deliver such effective service to the relatively concentrated group of corporations and individuals who own and control the major-league sports industry, its profitable synergy with the industry will continue apace. And this means the continued saturation of the sports pages with news about the big-time sports.

Indeed, sports journalism for the daily press is really no different than any other form of journalism appearing elsewhere in newspapers for special audiences. As Lawrence Wenner observes, there are many parallels to the entertainment, business, sports, and real-estate sections: there is an industry to be covered, a listing of major events, and stories about key players in that industry.[4] 'The section of the newspaper would not be there without the industry and, ultimately, a positive social take or fascination with the industry.' Thus, what is called 'real news' about that industry, whether it be a large embezzlement story in business or the arrest of a famous entertainer, often moves forward to the 'hard news' section. It's not often one finds a news item in the tourism section condemning Indonesia for its genocidal practices in East Timor over the past twenty years.

In this respect, the sports section of the daily newspaper, much like the entertainment or society pages – exists apart from 'real' or 'hard' news as a source of escape and pleasure. This is the sense of the old saying about the sports pages being the 'playpen' of the newspaper – what is reported here doesn't really matter because it's 'just' sports, what the late sportscaster Howard Cosell disparagingly called 'the toy department of life.' Only hard news stories merit attention. It follows that what is reported in the sports pages isn't really 'news' because real news is for the real-news section of the paper. What appears in the sports section, then, is rather innocuous regarding what matters in society – the sports section exists apart from real news as a fantasy world, one of pleasure and escape from everyday life, and it shouldn't be sullied with reportage critical of the major-league sports industry.

But there are exceptions to this pattern, as the *Globe and Mail's* Stephen Brunt, for example, regularly demonstrates with his rare brand of critical sportswriting. In a column about the upcoming 1996 Olympic Games in Atlanta, Brunt challenged city officials' claim that 'for many [Atlanta] is the modern capital of human rights.'[5] The reference was supposed to 'stir visions of Dr. Martin Luther King, of the city's place in the history of the civil rights movement, and in the process wipe out any lingering thoughts of the bad Old South.' Citing a major report by Human Rights Watch that was scheduled to be released before the Games' opening ceremonies, Brunt demonstrates how such a claim rings hollow in light of the documentary record on Atlanta and on Georgia as a whole. Among the abuses documented by Human Rights Watch, 'some of which are in violation of federal and state laws, the U.S. Constitution, and international human rights agreements signed by the U.S. government,' were the following:

- unjustified shootings and beatings by the Atlanta police, who are not subject to any kind of meaningful civilian review;
- capital punishment, including the execution of those who committed crimes as minors, and – until recently – of those who were mentally retarded;
- drug laws that are enforced disproportionately against blacks, just as a disproportionate number of blacks are executed;
- conditions so terrible in state prisons that the U.S. government has threatened to sue eleven Georgia counties over the state of their jails;
- sexual harassment and intimidation of women prisoners, including rape by jail guards;
- cruel restraint and punishment of minors held in custody;
- discrimination against gay men and lesbians.[6]

This is the sort of journalism we find too rarely in the sports pages. But why bring up human rights issues and the like in the guise of sports news; aren't such issues better left to the 'hard news' section? And in any case, why bring all this up in the weeks leading up to the beginning of the centennial Olympic Games? Is there anything to be gained thereby?

Just before the start of the Games was precisely the crucial time to raise such questions. In Brunt's words, 'Now, because any other time, without the Olympic spotlight, no one would give a damn. If the [Human Rights Watch] report had been released a year ago, two years ago, or even when the bidding process was taking place, it would have disappeared pretty much without comment.'

In the regular course of events, critical coverage of sports, especially major-league sports, is not meant for the sports section (it is not too much of a leap to argue that it's not meant for the daily newspaper *at all*, or the mainstream media for that matter). What is important to draw from Brunt's comments is that it takes a major entertainment spectacle like the Olympics to open a window of opportunity for journalists to ram through truly critical news items on the world of major-league sports. Otherwise it's business as usual, with 'criticism' confined to the banal. Again, the reason for this is simple – the sports section exists to promote sports entertainment spectacle.

It is precisely this promotional discourse that makes major-league sport so ideologically charged. As Richard Gruneau and David Whitson argue, the popular discourses produced around sport in the mass media work more to sustain than to challenge the new economic and political orthodoxies of the 1990s.[7] For example, I want to take up briefly their suggestion that the vast majority of what people have read and heard about trade unions in recent years has probably come from the 'intense media coverage of the recent strikes and lockouts in hockey and baseball.' Gruneau and Whitson argue that these sports 'unions' function in a vastly different fashion from most trade unions. Professional sports unions negotiate collective agreements that set the framework within which individual 'workers' negotiate private contracts – rather than 'negotiating collective agreements whose wage scales and agreements on work conditions, benefits, and so on are felt *collectively* across an industry or workplace.' Moreover, other unions engage in distincly 'political work,' underpinned by a sense of solidarity, of a collective sense of 'we're in this together' – a feeling that is not even remotely a guiding principle of professional-sports unionism. Yet these differences get lost in media coverage of labour disputes in sports. Meanwhile, Gruneau and Whitson argue, populist anger at the actions of 'greedy' players who already make huge salaries 'seems easily extended to a tacit condemnation of trade unionism in general' – certainly one of the prevailing currents of popular neo-liberal thought nowadays.

In our age of debt and deficit mania, the need to exercise greater labour discipline is a corporate mantra. We're told that to turn around sagging economies we must cut not only the size of government at all levels but also spending on social programs of various sorts. What is interesting to note is that the powerful corporate interest groups that are lobbying incessantly to dismantle the welfare state are the biggest lobbyists for the public financing of professional sports franchises and brand-new sports stadiums. Since the late 1960s, most professional sports teams have played in publicly subsidized facilities.[8] Calgary's Saddledome, the Northlands Coliseum in Edmonton, Olympic Stadium in Montreal, Toronto's SkyDome – all are spectacular instances of the socialization of major-league sport, of the public underwriting of the awesome costs of major entertainment infrastructures.

That there is no sustained critique of this state of affairs in the sports pages attests to the abilities of the corporate interests that control major-league sports to promote their interests as more legitimate and prestigious than those of others.[9] The economic logic of the sports news business compels editors to fill their sports pages with staggering quantities of major-league sports news every day – but not of the critical sort, nothing that would consistently call into question the sports entertainment industry.

But, really, this shouldn't be so surprising. Were journalists to challenge this state of affairs they wouldn't be fulfilling their role as head cheerleaders for the major-league sports business. Remember, it is their job to 'keep the dream alive' – to construct an imaginary 'us' around major-league sports. They exhort local citizens to support 'their' team by buying seasons tickets and so on, 'as if everyone shares in the benefits [professional sports teams] bring to their "home" cities.'[10] Even skyrocketing ticket costs should not be seen as a barrier to performing this vital civic duty, a point the *Vancouver Sun* drives home (with powerful subtlety) in a 'Special Report' on the costs of professional sports.[11] Despite the report's pretensions to being a serious investigative series on the major-league sports industry, however, one quickly gets the sense that there is a major ticket drive happening here and little else. The final instalment of the series, titled 'It Comes Down to the FANS,' merits special attention in this regard.

The main theme is that the average fan really can afford the escalating costs – you just have to be a little creative, that's all. If you aren't, no fear, because the 'report' offers advice on how the average fan can 'get a piece of the action.' For those finding it increasingly difficult to afford a night at General Motors Place watching the Canucks or the Grizzlies, there is always the option of ticket sharing, one article informs us. A second article suggests that fans can just 'bite the bullet' and shell out the money; after all, 'There's no use saving all this money and then dying before you can spend it.' And besides, as one fan explained, 'If we start to say how much is worth per minute, [the cost] starts to come down substantially. You do get 60 minutes of action. What does it cost you? A buck and a quarter a minute, less than a buck, I guess. There's a lot of people who spend a buck and a quarter for a lot less than we get here.'

Apparently for the *Vancouver Sun* the cost of professional sports is *not* too high: regular folks just have to make some sacrifices if they want to enjoy the 'benefits' of living in a 'world class' city like Vancouver. One Vancouver Canucks season-ticket holder put this into perspective when asked by a reporter to comment on the opening of General Motors Place: 'It's a building designed to make money from people for people who have money.'[12]

The sports pages are *about* major-league spectator sports. Sportswriters and editors, athletes, team owners, media commentators, civic boosters – they all routinely *define* sports news as news about a handful of male-dominated professional sports. The practices and routines that reporters follow in casting the news net and producing the sports section enable the daily realization of that definition.[13] The economic logic of the sports-news business virtually precludes coverage of anything but intense entertainment spectacles.

Ottawa Sun sports editor Tim Baines put it best when he commented, in the wake of the 1994 labour strife in professional sport: 'Hopefully we haven't covered amateur sports so much that people will expect it to continue at this level, because this'll never happen again.'[14]

Interview Questions

Throughout my fieldwork I carried with me three basic interview schedules, each designed for one of the three major occupational groups under study: sportswriters, editors, and media relations staffers for major-league sports organizations. These are reproduced below. As I noted earlier in chapter 2, these interview schedules were used only as guides; they were not rigorously adhered to, as required in proper survey interview techniques. I wanted to provide interviewees with minimal guidance, allowing considerable latitude to explore new avenues opened during the course of an interview; sometimes these were dead ends, and at other times important insights were yielded.

Sportswriters

How long have you been a sportswriter? How many years at the *Examiner* specifically?

Do you have any experience covering other types of news, such as city/regional politics, business or foreign affairs? If so, do you see any parallels between covering them and covering sports?

Have you any experience other than sports reporting, say as an editor or desker or in some other job in the newsroom?

What level of education do you have? Does this include any professional training in a journalism program in college and/or university?

Tell me about the difference between working a designated sports beat and working as a 'general assignment' reporter or as a 'freelancer,' if there is a difference.

Is working a beat more prestigious?

What about columnists? How does their work differ from covering a beat?

Tell me about a typical day working as a sports reporter for the *Examiner*.

What kinds of pressures and constraints do you work under every day? How do these impact your daily work routines?

How many stories do you write in a typical day? Is there a set number your editor expects from you?

I want to know more about sports news sources. Give me some examples of who is a news source, someone you regularly go to.

Are some sources more important to you than others? Why (or, why not)?

How important are your sources to your work?

A number of sports journalists have talked about how various sources try to influence what gets reported in the sports pages – this is especially the case with media relations staffers, but also athletes and coaches and management types. They only want 'positive' things written about themselves and their sport. Tell me about this state of affairs.

What about 'sanctions' as a means by which routine sources try to control what becomes sports news? Have you ever personally experienced these? Do you know of others who have?

In what ways do sources sanction reporters who have upset them?

Do you think these sanctions really have an impact on content in the sports pages? Do they have a real, tangible impact on your work?

Have you ever not written a story or suppressed elements of a story that might have offended one of your routine sources?

Sports Editors

Tell me about your background, in terms of education and years of actual working experience.

How long have you worked specifically as a sports editor? How many years at the *Examiner*?

Tell me about your job. What do you do in a typical day, from start to finish?

I want to know more about the newsroom environment here at the *Examiner*. What sort of pressures and constraints do you face in putting your sports section together each day?

How does story assignment work? Do you assign reporters to cover specific events, or do they just go out on their own and turn in their stories at the end of the day? In this sense, how do you as editor (or assistant editor) decide what gets covered and what doesn't?

Do your reporters have to generate a specific number of stories each day, in the sense of a rigid quota?

Tell me how a sports beat works. What kind of resources does it take to cover a beat?

What about advertising? How does it influence the sports pages in terms of content – that is, in terms of the types of sports covered and *not* covered?

How does advertising affect the amount of space given on a daily basis to major-league sports versus more non-commercial sports, especially community-based sports?

It has been suggested that sports news is so much about professional sports because this is the kind of news coverage that attracts a predominantly *male* readership, which is so appealing to advertisers. To what extent is this the case?

How do you specifically target male readers? How do you attract and hold them over long periods of time?

Where do non-commercial sports fit into your coverage strategies?

How do community sports rank in terms of importance compared to the local professional sports teams?

Why does there seem to be so little really critical journalism in the sports pages of daily newspapers? By 'critical' I mean the sort of investigative reporting characteristic of the political and business sections of the paper.

Do you think that sports journalism is different from political or business journalism?

To what extent do you think sports reporters have a social obligation to report critically on sports, to go beyond the prevailing model of just reporting what happens in professional sports?

Media Relations Staffers

How would you characterize your job? In what terms?

What does media relations work entail on a daily basis?

At a more general level, a macro level, what are the objectives of doing media relations work for a professional sports organization?

What strategies do you employ to meet your promotional objectives?

I've read in a number of studies of media relations work in large bureaucracies that the key to doing effective media relations is to facilitate newswork, that is, help journalists do their work. To what extent does this apply to doing media relations for a sports organization?

What do you do to facilitate the work of sports reporters, to make it easier for them to do their job? What kinds of services and facilities do you provide reporters?

How effective are press releases and news conferences to your promotional efforts?

How do you handle a situation where one of your athletes or coaches gets into some sort of trouble that could harm the team's image? For example, a star athlete caught using illegal drugs or gambling?

What do you do with a reporter who is consistently critical of your organization?

In terms of facilitating sports newswork, would you ever 'cut off' a reporter whom you think is over-critical, in terms of their coverage of your team and its players, coaches, and management?

Notes

Introduction

1 S. Gardener, 'During the recent hockey lockout, some editors found other ways to fill pages,' *Media*, March 1995, 6–7, 22.
2 R. Ericson, P. Baranek, and J. Chan, *Representing Order* (Toronto: University of Toronto Press, 1991), 16.
3 To protect anonymity as much as possible, all individuals and organizations in the 'Big City' community have been given pseudonyms. The *Examiner* is a tabloid-format daily, and at the time of study had a weekly (Monday to Friday) circulation of 52,290 readers in a market area of approximately 710,000 adults over the age of 18 years (*Canadian Advertising Rates and Data*, June 1994).
4 A. Giddens, *Sociology: A Brief but Critical Introduction* (New York: Harcourt, Brace, Jovanovich, 1982), 10. See also R. Gruneau and D. Whitson, *Hockey Night in Canada* (Toronto: Garamond, 1993), 34.
5 L.V. Sigal, *Reporters and Officials* (Lexington, Mass.: D.C. Heath, 1973), 101.
6 M. Fishman, *Manufacturing the News* (Austin: University of Texas Press, 1980), 13.
7 B. Glasser and A. Strauss, *The Discovery of Grounded Theory* (Chicago: Aldine, 1967).
8 B. McFarlane, 'The Sociology of Sports Promotion,' unpublished master's thesis, McGill University, Montreal, 1955; G. Smith, 'A Study of a Sports Journalist,' *International Review for the Sociology of Sport*, 1976; R. Telander, 'The Written Word: Player-Press Rela-

tionships in American Sports,' *Sociology of Sport Journal* 1 (1984), 3–14; N. Theberge and A. Cronk, 'Work Routines in Newspaper Sports Departments and the Coverage of Women's Sports,' *Sociology of Sport Journal* 3 (1986), 195–203; M. Lowes, 'Sports Page: A Case Study in the Manufacture of Sports News for the Daily Press,' *Sociology of Sport Journal* 14:2 (1997), 143–59.

Chapter 1: Selling Spectacle

1 D. Beddoes, *Brief Submitted to the Special Senate Committee on the Mass Media.* 28th Parliament, 2nd Session, 1970, vol. 24, 66.
2 Ibid., 66; emphasis added.
3 L. Koppett, *Sports Illusion, Sports Reality* (Boston: Houghton Mifflin, 1981), 101.
4 L. Wenner, ed., *Media, Sports, and Society* (Thousand Oaks, Calif.: Sage, 1989), 15.
5 F. Cosentino, *A Passing Game: A History of the CFL* (Winnipeg: Bain & Cox, 1995), 217.
6 Ibid., 226.
7 Koppett, *Sports Illusion, Sports Reality*, 11; my emphasis.
8 J. Stevens, 'The Rise of the Sports Page,' *Gannett Center Journal* 1:2 (Fall 1987), 10; my emphasis.
9 P. Rutherford, *The Making of the Canadian Media* (Toronto: McGraw Hill–Ryerson, 1978), 49.
10 Ibid., 49.
11 Gruneau and D. Whitson, *Hockey Night in Canada*, 82.
12 W. Leiss, S. Kline, and S. Jhally, *Social Communication in Advertising*, 2nd ed. (Scarborough: Nelson, 1990), 102.
13 M. Vipond, *The Mass Media in Canada* (Toronto: James Lorimer & Co., 1992), 13.
14 J. Coakley, *Sport in Society* (St Louis: Times-Mirror / Moseby College Publishing, 1986), 95.
15 J. Lever and S. Wheeler, 'The Chicago Tribune Sports Page, 1900–1975,' *Sociology of Sport Journal* 1 (1984), 299–313.
16 Rutherford, *The Making of the Canadian Media*, 60.
17 Ibid., 60–1.
18 Gruneau and Whitson, *Hockey Night in Canada*, 83.

19 Ibid. See also the excellent discussion of this topic in B. Kidd, *The Struggle for Canadian Sport* (Toronto: University of Toronto Press, 1996), esp. 14–18.

20 R. Sparks, 'Delivering the Male: Sports, Canadian Television, and the Making of TSN,' *Canadian Journal of Communication* 17 (1992), 319–42.

21 Wenner, *Media, Sports, and Society*, 36.

22 T.J. Scanlon, 'Sports in the Daily Press in Canada,' Report prepared for the Directorate of Fitness and Amateur Sport, Department of National Health and Welfare (Ottawa, 1970).

23 M. Gelinas and N. Theberge, 'A Content Analysis of the Coverage of Physical Activity in Two Canadian Newspapers,' *International Review for the Sociology of Sport* 21 (1986), 141–51.

24 Coakley, *Sport in Society*, 102; see also J. Bryant, 'A Two-Year Selective Investigation of the Female in Sport as Reported in the Paper Media,' *Arena Review* 4:2 (1980).

25 Gardener, 'During the recent hockey lockout,' 7.

26 Ibid.

27 Sparks, 'Delivering the Male.'

28 Ibid., 319.

29 Ibid., 333.

30 Ibid., 335.

Chapter 2: Inside the Newsroom

1 R. Cavanagh, 'Cultural Production and the Reproduction of Power: Political Economy, Public Television and High Performance Sport in Canada,' unpublished doctoral dissertation, Carleton University, Ottawa, 1989, 218–21.

2 Biographical information is not available for Jill, as she was on vacation when I was collecting this data. This is also the case with Bobby Barnes.

3 Interestingly, during my first visit to the paper, when the local 6:00 p.m. news broadcast came on air, someone (I later learned it was the city editor) barked, 'Who's got the news?' A reporter shouted back, 'I do,' and, with pen and pad in hand, took notes on the broadcast.

Chapter 3: Working the Sports Beat

1 G. Tuchman, *Making News* (New York: Free Press, 1978), 144.
2 Ibid. Note that Nancy Theberge and Alan Cronk likewise employ this analogy in their study of sports newswork, 'Work Routines in Newspaper Sports Departments,' 198
3 Tuchman, *Making News*, 21.
4 Fishman, *Manufacturing the News*, 35.
5 Ibid.
6 L. Shecter, *The Jocks*, 12.
7 C. Cumming and C. McKercher, *The Canadian Reporter* (Toronto: Harcourt Brace & Co. Canada, 1994), 292.
8 Ibid., 293.
9 T. Frayne, *The Tales of an Athletic Supporter* (Toronto: McClelland & Stewart, 1990), 308.
10 Koppett, *Sports Illusion, Sports Reality*, 112.

Chapter 4: The Routine Sources of Sports News

1 R. Ericson, P. Baranek, and J. Chan, *Negotiating Control: A Study of News Sources* (Toronto: University of Toronto Press, 1989).
2 McFarlane, 'The Sociology of Sports Promotion,' 152.
3 Ibid., 65.
4 This summary is drawn from Koppett, *Sports Illusion, Sports Reality*, 146–7.
5 L.V. Sigal, *Reporters and Officials*, 104.
6 Fishman, *Manufacturing the News*, 152.
7 McFarlane, 'The Sociology of Sports Promotion,' chap. 4.
8 Beddoes, *Brief on the Mass Media*, 64–75. This committee was an inquiry by the Canadian federal government into the growing concentration of ownership in the Canadian media industry, especially the daily press. It was followed up only eleven years later, in 1981, with the Royal Commission on Newspapers, which likewise was motivated by the alarming growth in ownership concentration. And in June 1996, there were calls for yet another commission of inquiry as a result of Conrad Black's recent buying spree of English dailies in Canada. At this time Black controls 58 of Canada's 104

dailies, including papers in Ottawa and five provincial capitals. Together they account for about 41 per cent of the newspaper copies sold each day in Canada.

9 G. Smith, 'A Study of a Sports Journalist,' *International Review for the Sociology of Sport*, 1976, 15.

10 It would be instructive to conduct further research on this matter. For example, obtaining a number of press releases and comparing them to the corresponding news items published in the *Examiner* over a period of time (essentially a content analysis) could provide valuable insight into the extent to which newsworkers rewrite releases as news items.

11 This material is drawn from a *Vancouver Sun* article comparing General Motors Place to the old Pacific Coliseum – how GM Place is a great deal more 'media friendly' (15 Sept. 1995: C14).

12 'Racial tension a stark reality in pro sports,' *Globe and Mail*, 13 Dec. 1997, A28.

13 Fishman, *Manufacturing the News*, 37–44.

14 'The death of sportswriting,' *The World*, 20 Oct. 1991.

15 This notion of 'idealization' is drawn from Fishman, *Manufacturing the News*, chap. 2.

16 Telander, 'The Written Word,' 4.

Chapter 5: Reporter and Source Relations

1 A. Wernick, *Promotional Culture* (London: Sage, 1991).

2 Gruneau and D. Whitson, *Hockey Night in Canada*, 137–8.

3 Ibid., 138.

4 Leo Rosten, *The Washington Correspondents* (New York: Harcourt, Brace, 1937), 73. It should be noted that Rosten was writing about political administrations, but his point is easily extended to business organizations like professional sports teams.

5 Gare Joyce, 'One big job, two different approaches,' *Globe and Mail*, 2 Nov. 1996.

6 Telander, 'The Written Word.' (1984), pp. 3–14.

7 D. Beddoes, *Brief on the Mass Media*, 70.

8 Cumming and McKercher, *The Canadian Reporter*, 296.

9 Beddoes, *Brief on the Mass Media*, 65.

10 Beddoes, *Pal Hal* (Markham: Penguin Books, 1989), 262.
11 Telander, 'The Written Word,' 4.
12 Richman,'The death of sportswriting,' 7–8, 10–11.
13 Marty York, 'Familiar refrain echoes in CFL,' *Globe and Mail*, 3 July 1996.
14 As a point of interest, Chet Burkley offered this observation on the team's actions: 'Consequently we don't go on the road with them anymore as much as we used to, it would cost us too much. So they don't get as much coverage and it just hurts them in the long run.'
15 Koppett, *Sports Illusion, Sports Reality*, 97.
16 'Racial tension a stark reality in pro sports,' *The Globe and Mail*, 13 Dec. 1997: A28.
17 Telander, 'The Written Word,' 4.
18 *Globe and Mail*, 6 Oct. 1994, A17.
19 Ibid., 18 Jan. 1995, A15.
20 G. Smith and T. Valeriote, 'Ethics in Sports Journalism,' in E. Lapchick, ed., *Fractured Focus* (Lexington, Mass.: Lexington Books, 1986), 323.
21 Beddoes, *Pal Hal*, 263.
22 Cited in Robert Stebbins, *Canadian Football: The View from Inside the Helmet* (London: Centre for Social and Humanistic Studies, U of Western Ontario, 1987), 154.
23 Although I would not characterize Canadian university football as 'major league,' I do regard coach Krusher as a routine news source because not only is he the head coach of a major university football program in Big City but, more important, he is a frequent guest coach with Big City's CFL team. Plus, he has coached a number of professional football players, and is thus a frequent news source for local sports journalists who regularly ask him for comment.
24 Koppett, *Sports Illusion, Sports Reality*, 100.

Chapter 6: In Whose Interests?

1 Cited in Fishman, *Manufacturing the News*, 134. Gaye Tuchman, in *Making News*, also describes the manner in which various news-work practices are a 'means not to know': 'The temporal and spatial anchoring of the news net ... prevents some ... occurrences from

being defined and disseminated as news. Professional practices ... dismiss some analyses of social conditions as soft news novelties and transform others into ameliorative tinkerings with the status quo' (180).

2 John B. Thompson, *Studies in the Theory of Ideology* (Cambridge: Cambridge University Press, 1984), 4.

3 Terry Eagleton, *Ideology: An Introduction* (London: Verso, 1991), 58–60.

4 L. Wenner, 'Drugs, Sport, and Media Influence,' *Journal of Sport and Social Issues* 18:3 (August 1994), 285.

5 Stephen Brunt, 'The flip side of Georgia's Olympic image,' *Globe and Mail*, 13 July 1996.

6 These are quoted directly from the Brunt article.

7 D. Whitson and R. Gruneau, 'The (Real) Integrated Circus: Political Economy, Popular Culture, and "Major League" Sport,' in W. Clement, ed., *Building on the New Canadian Political Economy* (Montreal: McGill-Queen's University Press, 1997), 33–4. I am grateful to Rick Gruneau for not only providing me with a draft copy of this chapter, but for elaborating on its more theoretical points concerning the production of popular discourses around major-league sport.

8 Ibid., 19.

9 See Richard Gruneau, 'The Politics and Ideology of Active Living,' in James Curtis and Storm Russell, eds, *Social Approaches to Active Living* (Urbana, Ill.: Human Kinetics Press, 1996), 2–3.

10 Whitson and Gruneau, 'The (Real) Integrated Circus,' 34.

11 Pete McMartin and Gary Kingston, 'Pro sports: Too high a price?' *Vancouver Sun*, 9, 11, 12 Sept. 1995.

12 *Globe and Mail*, 23 Sept. 1995.

13 Theberge and Cronk, 'Work Routines in Newspapers Sports Departments.'

14 Quoted in Gardener, 'During the recent hockey lockout,' 22.

References

Bagdikian, Ben. *The Media Monopoly.* 4th ed., Boston: Beacon Press, 1992.

Beamish, Rob. 'Materialism and the Comprehension of Gender-Related Issues in Sport.' In Nancy Theberge and Peter Donnelly, eds, *Sport and the Sociological Imagination.* Fort Worth: Texas Christian University Press, 1984.

Beddoes, Dick. *Brief Submitted to the Special Senate Committee on the Mass Media.* 28th Parliament, 2nd Session, 1970, vol. 24, 64–75.

Bryant, James. 'A Two-Year Selective Investigation of the Female in Sport as Reported in the Paper Media.' *Arena Review* 4:2 (1980).

Canadian Advertising Rates and Data, 67:6 (June 1994). Maclean Hunter Publishing: Toronto.

Cavanagh, Richard P. 'Cultural Production and the Reproduction of Power: Political Economy, Public Television and High Performance Sport in Canada.' Unpublished doctoral dissertation, Carleton University, Ottawa, 1989.

Chomsky, Noam, and Edward Herman. *Manufacturing Consent.* New York: Pantheon Books, 1988.

Coakley, Jay. *Sport in Society.* St Louis: Times-Mirror / Moseby College Publishing, 1986.

Cosentino, Frank. *A Passing Game: A History of the CFL.* Winnipeg: Bain & Cox, 1995.

Cumming, Carman, and Catherine McKercher. *The Canadian Reporter.* Toronto: Harcourt Brace and Co. Canada, 1994.

Ericson, Richard, Patricia Baranek, and Janet Chan. *Representing Order.* Toronto: University of Toronto Press, 1991.

– *Negotiating Control: A Study of News Sources.* Toronto: University of Toronto Press, 1989.

– *Visualizing Deviance: A Study of News Organization.* Toronto: University of Toronto Press, 1987.

Fishman, Mark. *Manufacturing the News.* Austin: University of Texas Press, 1980.

Frayne, Trent. *The Tales of an Athletic Supporter.* Toronto: McClelland & Stewart, 1990.

Gantz, Walter. 'Exploring the Role of Television in Married Life.' *Journal of Broadcasting and Electronic Media* 29 (1985), 263–75.

Gantz, Walter, and Lawrence Wenner. 'Fanship and the Television Sports Viewing Experience.' *Sociology of Sport Journal* 12 (1995), 56–73.

– 'Men, Women, and Sports: Audience Experiences and Effects.' *Journal of Broadcasting and Electronic Media* 35 (1991), 233–43.

Gardener, Sue. 'During the recent hockey lockout, some editors found other ways to fill pages.' *Media,* March 1995, 6–7, 22.

Gelinas, M., and N. Theberge. 'A Content Analysis of the Coverage of Physical Activity in Two Canadian Newspapers.' *International Review for the Sociology of Sport* 21 (1986), 141–51.

Giddens, Anthony. *Sociology: A Brief but Critical Introduction.* New York: Harcourt, Brace, and Jovanovich, 1982.

Glasser, Barney, and Anselm Strauss. *The Discovery of Grounded Theory.* Chicago: Aldine, 1967.

Gruneau, Richard. 'Making Spectacle: A Case Study in Television Sports Production.' In L. Wenner, ed., *Media, Sports, & Society.* Thousand Oaks, Calif.: Sage, 1989.

Gruneau, Richard, and David Whitson. *Hockey Night in Canada.* Toronto: Garamond Press, 1993.

Jhally, Sut. 'The Spectacle of Accumulation: Material and Cultural Factors in the Evolution of the Sports/Media Complex.' *Insurgent Sociologist* 12:33 (1984), 41–57.

Kidd, Bruce. *The Struggle for Canadian Sport.* Toronto: University of Toronto Press, 1996.

Koppett, Leonard. *Sports Illusion, Sports Reality*. Boston: Houghton Mifflin, 1981.

Leiss, William, Stephen Kline, and Sut Jhally. *Social Communication in Advertising*. 2nd ed. Scarborough, Ont.: Nelson, 1990.

Lever, Janet, and Stanton Wheeler. 'The Chicago Tribune Sports Page, 1900–1975.' *Sociology of Sport Journal* 1 (1984), 299–313.

Lowes, Mark. 'Sports Page: A Case Study in the Manufacture of Sports News for the Daily Press.' *Sociology of Sport Journal* 14:2 (1997), 143–59.

– 'Sports Page: Newswork Routines and the Social Construction of Sports News in the Daily Press.' Unpublished master's thesis, Carleton University, Ottawa, 1995.

McFarlane, Bruce 'The Sociology of Sports Promotion.' Unpublished master's thesis, McGill University, Montreal, 1955.

Parente, Donald. 'The Interdependence of Sports and Television.' *Journal of Communication* 27:3 (1977), 131–5.

Richman, Alan. 'The death of sportswriting.' *The World*, 20 October 1991, 7–8, 10–11.

Rintala, Janet, and Susan Birrell. 'Fair Treatment for the Active Female: A Content Analysis of Young Athlete Magazine.' *Sociology of Sport Journal* 1:3 (1984), 231–50.

Rutherford, Paul. *The Making of the Canadian Media*. Toronto: McGraw Hill–Ryerson, 1978.

Scanlon, T. Joseph. 'Sports in the Daily Press in Canada.' Report (unpublished) prepared for the Directorate of Fitness and Amateur Sport, Department of National Health and Welfare, Canada, 1970.

Shecter, Leonard. *The Jocks*. New York: Paperback Library, 1969.

Sigal, Leon V. *Reporters and Officials*. Lexington, Mass.: D.C. Heath, 1973.

Smith, Garry. 'A Study of a Sports Journalist.' In *International Review for the Sociology of Sport*, 1976, 5–24.

Smith, Garry, and Terry Valeriote. 'Ethics in Sports Journalism.' In Edward Lapchick, ed., *Fractured Focus*. Lexington, Mass.: Lexington Books, 1986.

Sparks, Robert. 'Delivering the Male: Sports, Canadian Television, and the Making of TSN.' *Canadian Journal of Communication* 17 (1992), 319–42.

Stevens, John. 'The Rise of the Sports Page.' *Gannett Center Journal* 1:2 (Fall 1987).

Telander, Rick. 'The Written Word: Player-Press Relationships in American Sports.' *Sociology of Sport Journal* 1 (1984), 3–14.

Theberge, Nancy, and Alan Cronk. 'Work Routines in Newspaper Sports Departments and the Coverage of Women's Sports.' *Sociology of Sport Journal* 3 (1986), 195–203.

Tuchman, Gaye. *Making News.* New York: Free Press, 1978.

Vipond, Mary. *The Mass Media in Canada.* Toronto: James Lorimer & Co., 1992.

Wenner, Lawrence, ed. *Media, Sports, & Society.* Newbury Park, Calif.: Sage, 1989.

Wernick, Andrew. *Promotional Culture.* London: Sage, 1991.

Whitson, David, and Richard Gruneau. 'The (Real) Integrated Circus: Political Economy, Popular Culture, and "Major League" Sport.' In Wallace Clement, ed., *Building on the New Canadian Political Economy.* Montreal: McGill-Queen's University Press, 1997.

Index